I'm reminded of your authentic faith, which first lived in your grandmother Lois and your mother Eunice. I'm sure that this faith is also inside you.

2 Timothy 1:5 (CEB)

Royalties from this book will be donated to
United Methodist Committee on Relief

A BIBLE STUDY BY 14 UNITED METHODIST WOMEN ABOUT

14 WOMEN OF THE BIBLE

Her Faith Still Speaks

Women of the Bible Who Shape Our Faith

SHERI CARDER HOOD

EDITOR

Her Faith Still Speaks

Women of the Bible Who Shape Our Faith

books@marketsquarebooks.com
141 N. Martinwood, Suite 2 Knoxville, Tennessee 37923

ISBN: 979-8-9942008-1-0

Printed and Bound in the United States of America

Editor: Sheri Carder Hood

Cover Design: Kevin Slimp

Page Design: Carrie Rood

Post-Process Editor: Ashley Burton

Contents

CHAPTER ONE

The God of Hagar

By Melanie Tubbs

Scripture Lesson: Genesis 21:8-21

> *The boy grew and stopped nursing. On the day he stopped nursing, Abraham prepared a huge banquet. Sarah saw Hagar's son laughing, the one Hagar the Egyptian had borne to Abraham. So, she said to Abraham, "Send this servant away with her son! This servant's son won't share the inheritance with my son Isaac." This upset Abraham terribly because the boy was his son. God said to Abraham, "Don't be upset about the boy and your servant. Do everything Sarah tells you to do because your descendants will be traced through Isaac. But I will make of your servant's son a great nation too, because he is also your descendant." Abraham got up early in the morning, took some bread and a flask of water, and gave it to Hagar. He put the boy in her shoulder sling and sent her away. She left and wandered through the desert near Beer-sheba. Finally, the water in the flask ran out, and she put the boy down under one of the desert shrubs. She walked away from him about as far as a bow shot and sat down, telling herself, I can't bear to see the boy die. She sat at a distance, cried out in grief, and wept. God heard the boy's cries, and God's messenger called to Hagar from heaven and said to her, "Hagar! What's wrong? Don't be afraid. God had heard the boy's cries over there. Get up, pick up the boy, and take him by the hand because I will make of him a great nation." Then God opened her eyes, and she saw a well. She went over, filled the water flask, and gave the boy a drink. God remained with the boy; he grew up, lived in the desert, and became an expert archer. He lived in the Paran desert, and his mother found him an Egyptian wife.*

Genesis 21:8-21 (CEB)

Starting in Genesis Chapter 12, Abraham becomes the central character in the story of God's relationship with God's people. God first tells Abraham to leave everything he has ever known—taking all that he has and everyone in his household—and go to an unknown place where God is sending him. Abraham obeys. During a famine in this new location, he goes to Egypt to survive. There, he becomes fabulously wealthy by passing his wife off as his sister and allowing her to be taken into Pharaoh's harem. When God sends plagues on Pharaoh and his household for taking a married woman, Abraham is kicked out of Egypt and returns to the land of Canaan with his newly acquired wealth. God reaffirms God's promise to Abraham that he would have land, descendants, and blessings, but this seems unlikely because Abraham and his wife, Sarah, are far too old to have children.

After years without conceiving a child and in desperation for an heir, Sarah offers her Egyptian slave, Hagar, to Abraham as a concubine. In the ancient Near East, it was a culturally accepted practice for a barren wife to offer her female servant to her husband as a surrogate to produce an heir. Legal codes from Mesopotamia, such as the Code of Hammurabi (ca. 18th century BCE), include provisions for this kind of arrangement, under which a servant's child could legally belong to the wife of the household. While this may have secured the wife's status, it often left the surrogate woman in a vulnerable, unstable position, neither fully a wife nor merely a servant.

Hagar, a woman without rights or control over her own body, is given by Sarah to this much older man and has no choice in the matter. She is used to bear a child that

Sarah can legally claim as her own. Hagar is treated not as a person with agency but as a means to an end within a system where enslaved women have no say. But even though it is Sarah's decision to send Hagar to Abraham, when Hagar becomes pregnant, Sarah abuses Hagar so badly that this woman without choices feels her only option is to run away into a dangerous, unforgiving desert. God comes to Hagar in the wilderness and tells her to return to the clan so she will have resources and protection in the only way available to her. So she does as she is told. Hagar has a son and names him Ishmael. While Scripture continues to refer to her as Sarah's maidservant, her role in the household shifts significantly. Hagar is now the woman who has given Abraham, a very wealthy and powerful man, a male heir. This changes her social standing and gives her a kind of maternal authority in the family, even if not the formal status of a wife. That shift, real or perceived, proves much harder for Sarah to live with than she had imagined.

Wesleyan theology reminds us that God's grace is always at work, even before we recognize it. John Wesley called this prevenient grace, grace that goes before, seeking us out in our wilderness moments. When Hagar meets God in the desert, she isn't in a place of power, purity, or religious belonging. She is exploited, cast out, and seemingly forgotten. And yet God comes to her. This is the very nature of grace: not earned or controlled but freely offered. In speaking to Hagar, God affirms her humanity, her worth, and her future. God's vision of justice is made visible in this encounter: Hagar, the foreign slave woman, is *seen* by the living God, and that same grace still seeks out those our world tries to forget.

Hagar has always fascinated me. She is said to be an Egyptian woman, so we assume she came with Abraham and Sarah when they left Egypt. She may have been a gift to Sarah from Pharaoh as a way to make amends for adding her to his harem when he thought she was unmarried. That means Hagar knew about the ruse Abraham and Sarah had pulled with Pharaoh, passing Sarah off as Abraham's sister. Hagar knew Sarah had spent time in Pharaoh's harem—a fact that likely added to Sarah's discomfort.

When Hagar becomes pregnant, Sarah complains that Hagar looks down on her and doesn't treat her with the respect Sarah believes she deserves. I always wonder if that is just because Hagar is able to conceive and Sarah isn't, or if maybe there is a little bit of the "I know what you did" thing going on. Not only did Hagar know what Abraham and Sarah had done, but now Hagar is pregnant with Abraham's baby, something Sarah had never been able to do. Perhaps that's one reason Sarah reacts so harshly to Hagar, because Hagar knows things Sarah would rather forget. Even though Sarah holds power as the first wife of a wealthy man, Hagar represents a truth Sarah cannot control.

While Hagar is on the run in the wilderness, God speaks to her—and not just a little command. God has a pretty long conversation as far as conversations with God go. Not only does God tell Hagar that she is to return and put up with Sarah, but God also tells her that she will have a son whom she should name Ishmael, who will be the foundation of his own nation.

Scripture says Hagar answered God, called God by name, and declared God to be *El Roi*, the "God who sees me." This is a significant declaration, given that we know she is Egyptian and that Egyptians worship their own many gods. Yet, there in the desert, pregnant and on the run, Hagar names the God of Abraham the "God who sees me." God reaffirms the covenant with Abraham, promising him land, descendants, and blessings, and at this point in the story, after Ishmael has already been born, God tells Abraham that it will actually be Sarah who will bear the son of promise. God also informs Abraham not to worry because God will bless Ishmael as well. Later, God appears to Abraham again—this time in the form of three messengers—and tells him that Sarah, now ninety, is about to become pregnant. Sarah and Abraham laugh hard at this, but a year later, Sarah gives birth to a son and names him Isaac, meaning laughter.

A new heir born to Sarah and Abraham presents a problem for Hagar and Ishmael. Where did that leave Ishmael in Abraham's line? Sarah, a woman who spent ninety years unable to have a child and became so desperate for one that she sent another woman to her husband's bed to conceive, immediately becomes defensive, wanting to be certain that nothing interferes with the inheritance of her own son. Ishmael had once been the answer to Abraham and Sarah's prayers. Now Hagar and Ishmael are, at the very least, an intrusion and possibly even a threat.

Three years later, there is a big party celebrating the fact that Isaac has survived infancy and is old enough to be weaned. At the party, Sarah sees Ishmael—now a teenager—laughing. We often interpret this to mean that Ishmael was laughing at Isaac. Some scholars suggest that the detail about Ishmael mocking Isaac may reflect a later editorial addition, shaped by theological tensions between the descendants of Isaac and Ishmael. It may just have been that

Sarah saw Ishmael laughing and having a good time at the party, which annoyed her. But whatever the reason, Sarah sees Ishmael laughing and tells Abraham that both Hagar and Ishmael must go.

One has to wonder if Sarah has been looking for a reason to throw Hagar and Ishmael out ever since Isaac was born. The opportunity presents itself at the celebration of Isaac's weaning, and Sarah doesn't waste any time running to tell Abraham that Hagar, the slave woman, and her son must go. After all, Isaac has survived infancy, so their "backup plan"—Ishmael—is no longer needed. She may have feared that Ishmael's presence threatened Isaac's inheritance, and in Sarah's eyes, nothing mattered more than securing her son's future.

Abraham didn't want to send Hagar and Ishmael away. Scripture says the thought was very distressing to him. But God speaks to Abraham that night and tells him to do what Sarah says: "Send them out, and I will make a nation of Ishmael, too, because he is your son." Abraham gives Hagar a loaf of bread and a bottle of water the next morning and sends her and Ishmael away. Not a great send-off for your firstborn son. Hagar and Ishmael were said to be wandering about in the wilderness, a rough and unforgiving landscape.

It's important to note that by sending her servant to Abraham, Sarah initiated a process that altered Hagar's role in the household. While Hagar was never formally recognized as a wife, bearing Abraham's child would have elevated her in the eyes of the community—at least socially, if not legally. That new position, however precarious, made her more visible and possibly more threatening to Sarah. But here, when Sarah is feeling more confident and powerful after the birth of her own son, she refers to Hagar once again as "that slave woman." Sarah's words are purposeful, designed to strip away any status or legitimacy Hagar may have gained through bearing Abraham's child. By reducing her once more to the role of a servant, Sarah seeks to erase any potential claims Hagar or Ishmael might have in Abraham's household.

One has to wonder why this story is even included in the stories of Abraham. If Isaac is the promised son, why tell this side story about a son who will ultimately be cast out? Aside from a brief mention years later, when Ishmael is present with Isaac to bury their father and a short genealogy report of Ishmael's descendants, we hear no more of Ishmael's story in the Bible. So why include it at all? The story of Abraham sending away his firstborn son into the wilderness casts both him and Sarah in a complicated and morally troubling light. And to abandon family members, people under your care and responsibility, was actually more than immoral; it was also illegal in their culture. So why is it included in Scripture?

Once again alone and desperate, this time with her son, Hagar believes that she is about to witness the slow, painful death of Ishmael from exposure and lack of water. But just like when she ran into the desert while pregnant, God shows up to speak directly to her: "Hagar! What's wrong? Don't be afraid." God comforts Hagar, assures her that her son will become a great nation, and points her to a well, saving the lives of her and her son.

Even though Ishmael isn't the child who would carry forward God's covenant promises, God has a plan for Hagar and Ishmael—and we know this is true because we get the genealogy list after Abraham dies in Genesis 25. We also know that Ishmael must have stayed in touch with his half-brother, Isaac, since, in a world without Facebook or text messages, Ishmael is present to bury his father. And I'm guessing that Ishmael took very good care of his mother, Hagar, who had gone through so much. He lived to be 137 years old and had twelve sons.

In fact, maybe Hagar is the point of the story and not Ishmael. After all, even though the messengers who spoke to Abraham acknowledged that Sarah laughed, God never sought out Sarah to have a chat with her. But God speaks directly to Hagar, not once but twice. If face time with God is a mark of importance in the Bible, Hagar is one of the more important characters. So why Hagar?

The main theme of all the stories in Genesis is the fulfillment of God's promise to Abraham. But by including Hagar's story, we are reminded that God still remembers the rest of God's people. Throughout the story of God's chosen people, those in the direct line from Abraham through David and to Christ, are also included the stories of lesser players. The minor players. The sidenotes. No matter where their stories go, God is always with them. Jacob declares that he sees the face of God in his brother, Esau, whose birthright was stolen and replaced by the younger Jacob. Maybe there is more to the Bible than just the direct institutional chosen path; maybe sometimes the exiles and the sidenotes are the point.

God is the God of second sons, outcast relatives, the lost, and the enslaved. God is not just the God of the big names of the Bible, the heroes of our faith, but also of the side characters and the forgotten ones. So many people can find their own story in the story of Hagar. The exploited worker, the other woman, the second wife, the sex abuse survivor, the surrogate mom, the resident alien, the single mother, the homeless woman, the woman with no identity but the one she has in association with men. Do we, the church community, remember the Hagars in our stories? Do we see them in our neighborhoods? What about when you are the Hagar and not the Sarah? Or maybe even more importantly, what about when you are the Sarah, and the story is about how you treat the Hagars?

Hagar and Ishmael are cast out. And while God doesn't prevent that from happening, in the middle of the fear and brokenness of where they are, God meets them in the wilderness and provides care in the present and hope and prosperity in the future.

Humans bring distress and alienation, but God is ever-present—even in the margins. God is a way-maker and a provider for all those whom society casts out. God is at work among the forgotten and the outcasts. God holds up the refugees and makes a new way. God may guide the chosen through the central story of Scripture, but God also dwells with the forgotten and the cast out in their wilderness places.

No matter where you are, who is against you, or what your circumstances may be, God is still *El Roi*, "the God who sees me." This same God is revealed again in Jesus Christ, who continually moved toward the outcast and gave voice to the silenced. He spoke with the Samaritan woman at the well, praised the persistence of the Syrophoenician woman, and restored the dignity of those others cast aside. Hagar's story is not an isolated moment; it is part of the ongoing story of a God who sees, hears, and redeems, even—and especially—in the wilderness.

Prayer:

El Roi, God who sees us, meet us in our wilderness places. When we feel forgotten, displaced, or pushed to the margins, remind us that your grace goes before us and your care never fails. Give us eyes to see those we have overlooked and hearts shaped by your justice, mercy, and love. Amen.

Reflection Questions:

1. Have you ever been jealous of someone's joy? Sarah is angry because Ishmael is enjoying himself at HER son's party—how dare he? He should know his place. How does our jealousy impact our relationships and our ability, or inability, to be in relationship with God?

2. What do you think of when you hear the word "haughty"? Think of a time or situation where someone behaved unvirtuously because they believed themselves to be higher in station or class. In Sarah's case, she felt less than because she couldn't conceive, and once she does conceive, this new station comes with new power that she uses to cause harm. How do we react when we are privileged with power over someone else?

3. Who are some other people God has conversations with in the Bible? How do the conversation and the results of the conversation with Hagar compare to the other times God speaks to humans? Specifically, how do Hagar's conversations with God compare to the conversations God has with Abraham? With the Woman at the Well (John 4)?

4. Ishmael and Isaac bury their father together. We know nothing of the in-between time from being cast out to the burial. Much of our Christian faith is rooted in forgiveness and reconciliation. Is there someone in your life you've made peace with or a situation you look back on with regret because forgiveness didn't happen? How can remembering you are a worthy, redeemed, and loved child of God help you in your own relationships? What can the story of Abraham, Sarah, Isaac, Hagar, and Ishmael teach us about our relationships?

5. Has there been a time when you were exiled or cast out, possibly feeling profound despair or hopelessness, and God spoke to you in the wilderness? When have you felt alone, abandoned, or not seen, but God pointed you to a well?

About the Writer:

Melanie Tubbs is an ordained elder in the Arkansas Conference of The United Methodist Church. Melanie is a graduate of ILIFF School of Theology and taught history in high school and college before entering full-time ministry.

CHAPTER TWO

Holding On. Letting Go.

By M. Kathryn Armistead

Scripture Lesson: Exodus 2:1-4

> *Now a man from the house of Levi went and married a Levite woman. The woman conceived and bore a son, and when she saw that he was a fine baby, she hid him three months. When she could hide him no longer, she got a papyrus basket for him and plastered it with bitumen and pitch; she put the child in it and placed it among the reeds on the bank of the river. His sister stood at a distance, to see what would happen to him.*
>
> **Exodus 2:1-4 (NRSVue)**

Many of us recognize this biblical passage as the beginning of Moses's story—Moses, who will free his people from oppression and set them on a course to enter God's Promised Land. As we may remember, Pharaoh is threatened by the number of Hebrews in Egypt. Fearing that the Hebrews would overrun his Egyptians and drive him from power, Pharaoh decrees that all newborn Hebrew baby boys be killed. However, in this Scripture, we meet a mother who is determined to thwart Pharaoh's plans. She successfully hides her newborn baby boy until he is three months old. Then, with what has to be a heavy heart, she prepares a basket and sets the baby adrift in the river. Yet, knowing she is sending him into danger, she does her best to protect him by making the little basket as watertight and sturdy as possible.

Parenthood is full of tough and sometimes painful choices. It is a balancing act between holding on and letting go. The balance between keeping your child safe and allowing your child to venture out away from you, away from home, away from safety and security, into a dangerous world that is, too often, callous and uncaring. Nevertheless, if we choose to let our children go, we can also do our best to prepare them for what they will find. The night before I started kindergarten, my father took me into the kitchen so we could be alone. He sat at the table and positioned me in front of him. Then he showed me how to make a fist—hold my hand this way, put my thumb here so—if I needed to defend myself, I'd be ready. I asked him if he thought I'd really have to fight somebody, and he said, "The world is full of bullies, so you'd better know how to take a stand."

Looking back, I'm not sure where he thought I was going. It was only to the new school up the street, a few blocks over, and I'd get to walk there every day by myself. We lived in a safe neighborhood. I was looking forward to it. But to him, I was leaving the nest, and it was his duty to prepare me for whatever might happen. For him, a World War II veteran, the world was full of uncertainty, and people were only too eager to push others around and out of the way. Even though I really didn't think I'd have to fight anyone, I was truly touched by how much he loved me, because that is what he was trying to show.

Jochebed—we learn her name in Numbers 26:59—was sending her son into more than uncertainty. She knew that she might be sending him to his death. She could have held on to him and risked being discovered, but that would have sealed her son's fate. But to let him go and put him in the water? The Nile was full of crocodiles and snakes, and of course, there were Pharaoh's orders. But in letting go, Jochebed chose to trust God with her son's future. And she must have prayed mightily as she put that basket in the water. I often wonder what Jochebed called her baby in those prayers, what she named him. We know him only as "Moses"—the name Pharaoh's daughter gave him when her maids saved him from the water. But as he drifted and she cried and prayed, what did she call after him in her heart?

We all have said countless prayers for our children—as they turn away and get on the school bus for the first time, when they go to their first sleepover, when they ask for the car keys to go out with friends, when they stand at the altar and take marriage vows, when they become parents themselves. I remember the first time my older daughter took the car after getting her driver's license. We still laugh about it. But it was no laughing matter at the time. From the moment she drove out the driveway, I stood at the picture window in the living room, watching, waiting, praying to God that she would return safely. I didn't budge until she drove back in.

It is tempting to think that parenting is over when the kids grow up and have families of their own. But it's not. Some of us sometimes bite our tongue when a grandchild is disciplined or indulged. We'd never do that! Some of us delight in doing for our grandkids what we couldn't or wouldn't do for our own kids. Some of us are proud yet sad when our kids take jobs far away, meaning that we won't get to see them as often. Some of us grieve over what we consider to be unwise decisions and the consequences our children have to endure. Parenting is a lifetime commitment. The holding on and letting go continues.

Holding close and letting go. We hold our children close because we love them, and we let them go because we love them. They need to grow up and make their own decisions. Hold too close, and we risk smothering and suffocating them, robbing them of opportunities to learn, even if they have to learn from their mistakes. Let go too soon, and we risk them not being ready. With discernment, we hold them just close enough and let them go just far enough that they will have the wherewithal to go further, even if they leave us behind.

Children can't be secure enough to leave unless we have held them close. And they can only successfully venture into unknown territories if we let them go with confidence—our confidence in them—and with the confidence that comes from the faith that God will go with them. We cannot do it all. We can never prepare our child for everything that might happen. Life is too unpredictable. Every time my husband, kids, and I left my folks after visiting for the holidays, I could see the sadness on my mother's face, even as she smiled and waved from the back porch. But she never cried. According to her, she was happy for us to come and happy for us to go. That was a great gift. She never made me feel guilty for leaving and having my own life. She trusted that God would go with us. No one says parenting is easy. And no one says that kids will be grateful despite your best efforts.

But there is one kind of letting go that must feel similar to what Jochebed felt as she launched that little boat. Recently, my daughter was diagnosed with bile duct cancer, a rare cancer with a high recurrence rate. Currently, she is undergoing chemotherapy. It's up and down for everyone. Yet it is a miracle that our neighbor in Tennessee had worked with an eminent transplant doctor in New York, who, in turn, got her to the right doctor. It is a miracle that she lives close to a world-class hospital. It is a miracle that the surgeon got "clear margins," even after three tries and ten hours of surgery. It is a miracle that when they removed more of the liver than they originally thought they could, it grew back—so many miracles. We are grateful—humbled—as we continue to pray. The journey is far from over. Her father and I watch from afar, just as Jochebed must have watched. We desperately want to hold her close, even while recognizing that we have to let her go. Yet we also know that God has prepared the way. God is with her.

When Jochebed let Moses go, she had no idea what plans God had for him—how he would free their people, how God would use him to tell Pharaoh to let his people go. While Jochebed surely grieved, she also had confidence in God and God's plan for her son, as well as for herself and her family. Why else plaster the basket with bitumen and pitch, if it was hopeless? No, Jochebed had faith, and her faith inspired hope. She prepared the best she could and had confidence that God would do the rest.

God always goes with us, but God also goes before us, preparing the way. Jochebed put the basket in the water, but God, in a great act of prevenient grace, went before and guided it to the reeds near the shore—not just any reeds, but the ones near Pharaoh's daughter. God went before by preparing Pharaoh's daughter's heart to adopt a Hebrew baby boy.

Even if we turn our backs on God, God is faithful, just, and merciful. God still loves us. Like a good parent, God is always there holding us when we need it, preparing us for our future, and going with us as we seek new paths. God helps us grow in faith, hope, and the love of God, self, and others. As we read in Psalm 23, God not only goes before us, but God also walks with us, even through the valley of the shadow of death. God can help us know when to hold on and when to let go, how to be a good parent, and how to be a faithful follower of Jesus. And our faith will help us prayerfully discern, live with confidence, and guide others into a more hopeful future. This much is certain.

Prayer:

Dear God, we praise you for being our good and loving parent. You made us and all we have. You give us the glory of the sunrise and the contentment of the sunset. We know you are Lord of today and tomorrow—the present and the future. We need not fear, even when we can't see the way ahead or when what we see scares us. But sometimes trusting you is hard. We have faith, but there are times when it doesn't seem like enough. We have hope, but it's fleeting. We have love, but we still miss the mark. Give us the wisdom to seek you in all things. Give us the courage to run back to you when we go astray. Help us love you enough that we follow even when darkness threatens. Free us for joyful obedience and faithful living. In the holy name of Jesus, Amen.

Reflection Questions:

1. Share the story of your first day at kindergarten. Did someone take you? Did you ride a bus? Do you still know any of those who were in your class?

2. How does becoming a mother or father change a person?

3. In this Scripture, we learn about what Moses' mother did. Moses' father doesn't play a part in the story. What do you think his response was to what Jochebed did?

4. As we read the story, we learn later that Moses' sister, Miriam, followed the basket, because she was on hand and quick to tell Pharaoh's daughter where she could find a nurse for Moses, which turns out to be Moses' own mother. What do you think it was like for Jochebed to be reunited with her son, then have to send him away again, this time to live with Pharaoh's daughter's household?

5. What happens when parents hold their children too close? What happens when parents don't hold their children close enough, or they let go too soon?

6. Why is it so difficult for many of us to trust God?

7. Share a time when you felt that God held you, protected you, and/or prepared the way for you.

8. Share a time when you prepared the way for another person or when you protected someone.

9. Name someone or something you need to hold close or let go.

About the Writer:

Kathy Armistead, PhD is an author, consultant, and the managing editor of *Methodist Review.* A deacon in The United Methodist Church, Kathy was formerly the publisher at the General Board of Higher Education and Ministry of The United Methodist Church. She is the ghostwriter or development editor of more than 450 books.

CHAPTER THREE

Miriam and the Holy Reversal

By Rebekah Simon-Peter

Scripture Lesson: Exodus 2:1-10

> *Now a man of the tribe of Levi married a Levite woman, and she became pregnant and gave birth to a son. When she saw that he was a fine child, she hid him for three months. But when she could hide him no longer, she got a papyrus basket for him and coated it with tar and pitch. Then she placed the child in it and put it among the reeds along the bank of the Nile. His sister stood at a distance to see what would happen to him.*
>
> *Then Pharaoh's daughter went down to the Nile to bathe, and her attendants were walking along the riverbank. She saw the basket among the reeds and sent her female slave to get it. She opened it and saw the baby. He was crying, and she felt sorry for him. "This is one of the Hebrew babies," she said.*
>
> *Then his sister asked Pharaoh's daughter, "Shall I go and get one of the Hebrew women to nurse the baby for you?"*
>
> *"Yes, go," she answered. So the girl went and got the baby's mother. Pharaoh's daughter said to her, "Take this baby and nurse him for me, and I will pay you." So the woman took the baby and nursed him. When the child grew older, she took him to Pharaoh's daughter and he became her son. She named him Moses, saying, "I drew him out of the water."*
>
> **Exodus 2:1-10 (NIV)**

Born and raised Jewish, I've always been drawn to the story of Miriam. Long before I ever met Jesus and other New Testament figures—which didn't happen until I was nearly thirty—Miriam symbolized for me all that a person like me could be and do to bring about good in the world. A role model for girls, Miriam is not only a key figure in the Exodus story, but she is also the first female prophet named in the Bible. Known for her steady presence, insight, and leadership abilities, Miriam starts out unnamed and unassuming. She holds no title, and her future role in God's holy reversal is unknown. She is simply a girl by a river, identified only by her relationship as "his sister" (Exodus 2:4). Jewish tradition tells us she is Miriam, the older sister of Aaron and Moses.

As we enter the story, Miriam stands some distance from the water, watching her baby brother, nestled in a small papyrus basket, drifting among the reeds of the Nile.

The scene is striking. By Pharaoh's order, every Hebrew baby boy should be thrown into the Nile. Egypt's life-giving river has now become a deadly weapon against Israel. But Miriam's mother will not give up her son or obey Pharaoh. Instead, she places him *on* the water, not *in* it. The Hebrew word used here for basket, *tevah*, is the same word used for Noah's ark. Covered with tar and pitch, this tiny papyrus ark floats and protects her child. It offers hope of deliverance. Putting him in the river is not compliance or abandonment. It is resistance.

Miriam watches her brother bobbing on the water in this makeshift vessel. I can imagine her holding her breath, wondering what will happen. Is he safe? Will the river pull him into stronger currents? I can almost feel the tension. Then, during this moment of suspense, a new presence appears and shifts events entirely.

Suddenly, Pharaoh's daughter arrives to bathe in the river, her attendants in tow. Her appearance disrupts Miriam's careful watchfulness. Dread and hope battle in the air as the story veers from anxious waiting to a heart-pounding interruption.

Pharaoh's daughter and her entourage approach. Their arrival could bring danger or deliverance for the little ark. Will they see the basket? What will it mean if they do? These women belong to the household that ordered this baby's death.

"She saw the basket among the reeds and sent her female slave to get it" (Exodus 2:5, NIV). She opens the basket, finds a crying child, and compassionately calls out, "This is one of the Hebrew babies" (Exodus 2:6, NIV).

In this moment, Miriam could have let fear freeze her. She could have turned away, or hidden, or stayed silent. Instead, her fear gives way to courage, and she lets faith lead the way. Miriam steps forward and asks, "Shall I go and get one of the Hebrew women to nurse the baby for you?" (Exodus 2:7, NIV).

With this single, daring question, Miriam sets in motion a holy reversal. Pharaoh's daughter seals it: "Yes, go" (Exodus 2:8, NIV). With these simple words, Pharaoh's daughter defies her own father's order and ensures the holy reversal can play out. She even pays the Hebrew woman to care for a child meant to die. Talk about an unexpected, miraculous outcome!

Miriam's story shows that resistance isn't always loud or grand. It does not require big gestures or important players. Sometimes, a holy reversal starts with a sister's care, a young woman's curiosity, or a handmaid's compassion.

Unnamed figures—sister, daughter, female slave—set the end of Hebrew slavery in motion, without knowing it.

Because of this miracle, Moses—once destined for death—returns to his mother's arms, cradled by love and family. When he grows, she surrenders him again, this time to Pharaoh's daughter and Pharaoh's household. But even there, he is nurtured. The triumph at the river lingers in Moses; his sense of justice burns, a quiet rebellion nourished by Miriam's sisterly protection.

Years later, and with God's help, the plagues come and reveal a way out of slavery for the Hebrews. Moses then leads the people through the Sea of Reeds, marking a new phase of deliverance. This echoes the earlier Nile episode—again, water brings both danger and deliverance. And as before, Miriam is present, taking part in the final stages of this holy reversal. While the children of Israel pass through the sea on dry ground, Pharaoh's army is swept away by the waters. Songs of victory and salvation pour through Moses and the men.

After Moses finishes his song, Miriam doesn't stay silent or wait for direction. Instead, she once again chooses the path of daring. Guided by divine inspiration, she picks up her tambourine and echoes her brother's song as she leads the women in worship, dance, and music.

> *Sing to the Lord, for he has triumphed gloriously;*
> *horse and rider he has thrown into the sea.*
>
> **Exodus 15:21 (NRSV)**

What strikes me most is the presence of tambourines. Tambourines are not essential gear, especially when fleeing for your life. Maybe Miriam reminded the women they serve a God of reversals and must be ready for miracles.

When their escape is complete, tambourines in hand, the women's worship is full-bodied. It goes beyond words. For women who have known fear and loss, Miriam's song strikes a chord. The water was deliverance for them but death to their oppressors. Slavery is over; the weight of suffering is lifted.

Miriam's story of holy reversal comes full circle. What young Miriam began at the edge of the Nile River among the reeds with one daring and compassionate act is now completed many years later by the entire community at the edge of the Sea of Reeds. They are led by an adult Miriam, now seasoned and wise.

It is in this pivotal moment that Scripture now gives her full name: "Miriam the prophetess, the sister of Aaron" (Exodus 15:20, NRSV). Her title is earned, not honorary. Alongside Moses and Aaron, Miriam now receives spiritual authority, a divine calling, and the power to speak for God. She stands as a chosen leader in this miraculous movement, this holy reversal, this moment when the Lord has not only triumphed gloriously over Egypt, but over injustice and inhumanity itself.

As wise and caring as Miriam is, she is not perfect. She has flaws. After Israel's escape from Egypt, the people wandered in the desert for forty years. Jewish tradition says this is where they start to shed their slave mentality so they can enter the Promised Land truly free. The journey is long and trying. About two years into their journey, after meeting God at Mount Sinai, conflict arises. Motivated by jealousy, Miriam and Aaron speak against their brother, Moses, for marrying a Cushite woman, a member of a different people (Numbers 12:1-2). God calls out both Aaron and Miriam, but singles out Miriam. She develops a skin disease and must stay outside the camp for seven days. Though corrected by God, she is not abandoned by God or the community. The people wait for her recovery. No one breaks camp or moves on until Miriam is restored and rejoins them. Whether leading boldly or sidelined by jealousy, Miriam remains integral to her people.

Time passes again. Some thirty-eight years later, in the wilderness of Zin, during the first month of the fortieth year of their wandering, the Bible says that Miriam died and was buried there (Numbers 20:1). Her death brings change. The next sentence tells us, "Now there was no water for the community" (Numbers 20:2, NIV). According to Jewish tradition, a miraculous well—Miriam's well—accompanied the people in their wanderings but dried up upon her death. Miriam's death brings emotional and relational loss to the entire community. Since Moses was a baby, she gave steady support. She bolstered the community, especially her siblings, in their own leadership. Her absence is starkly felt. Shortly after she dies, both Aaron and Moses die as well.

Even now, Miriam—nurturer and leader, compassionate and courageous—lives on in memory. Her hope at the river, her fierce faith at the sea, her well of steady resilience in the community, flows like a current through countless generations. Whenever courage rises in the face of fear, Miriam's spirit stirs the waters again calling us to be kind and compassionate agents of holy reversal in our own time.

It's no accident that other biblical women associated with

holy reversals share Miriam's same name. Centuries later, a young woman from Nazareth named Mary (the anglicized name of Miriam), who had not yet been with her husband, would deliver a child named Jesus. Jesus would go on to deliver his people from sin to salvation.

Some thirty-three years later, two women named Mary would be the first to hear the Easter news of resurrection from death, "He's not here. He has risen!" (Matthew 28:6, NIV).

In all three stories, the seemingly unlikely become instruments of hope and deliverance, reminding us that each generation is called to join the continuing story of holy reversal.

The story of salvation *is* the story of holy reversals. In times when male dominance was a given, even to the point where the Bible leaves females unnamed, God uses those same girls and women to change the order of things, to participate in the miraculous, and to bring deliverance.

The powerful story of Miriam is personal to me. Long before I first heard the biblical stories of Miriam, another Miriam touched my life deeply. My maternal grandmother, Miriam Goldberg, was not only the matriarch of our family but also a builder of community and the go-to person for many in the Jewish community. She helped ease others' suffering by working with my grandfather to establish a hospital where marginalized Jewish people could give and receive quality care. She helmed the local community paper for decades, which kept people connected. She was a true well of love, kindness, and practical leadership. When she died at 100½ years old, an entire community felt her loss.

The figure of Miriam continues to inspire and challenge

women today. We live in a time when injustice and inhumanity are again shaping the way we live and the freedoms we have. Where authoritarian figures seek to impose cruelty, limit compassion, and punish open-mindedness. Where holy reversals are needed. It's at times like these that it's important to remember that the toppling of Pharaoh's entire hierarchy of fearful cruelty started with one sister's courage and daring.

Miriam is forever a figure of divine agency, showing how courage and compassion can upend cruelty and alter history. Miriam's legacy calls us to seek holy reversals in our own communities, so that we participate with God's great story of redemption.

Prayer:

God, you are a God of holy reversals. Show us how to participate in your divine calling for love, justice, and mercy. Grant us your courage, kindness, and compassion for the times we live in. Amen.

Reflection Questions:

1. Have you ever witnessed or been part of a holy reversal?

2. How is God prompting you to be compassionate and courageous?

3. Can you see aspects of Miriam in your own life?

About the Writer:

Rebekah Simon-Peter is a visionary leader, acclaimed author, and dynamic speaker dedicated to empowering individuals and faith communities to embrace their divine potential. She is the author of seven books, including *Believe Like Jesus, Forging a New Path,* and *Dream Like Jesus.* Rebekah challenges and inspires others to move beyond discipleship into apostleship—boldly co-creating miracles with God. After serving churches for twelve years, she has transformed the lives of thousands of leaders over the last twenty years through her workshops and teachings, including her award-winning church renewal program, Creating a Culture of Renewal®.

CHAPTER FOUR

The Daughters of Zelophehad

The Power to Change the Story

By Gina Anderson-Cloud

Scripture Lesson: Numbers 27:1-7

> *The daughters of Zelophehad, Hepher's son, Gilead's grandson, Machir's great-grandson, and Manasseh's great-great-grandson, belonging to the clan of Manasseh son of Joseph, came forward. His daughters' names were Mahlah, Noah, Hoglah, Milcah, and Tirzah. They stood before Moses, Eleazar the priest, the chiefs, and the entire community at the entrance of the meeting tent and said, "Our father died in the desert. He wasn't part of the community who gathered against the Lord with Korah's community. He died for his own sin, but he had no sonsWhy should our father's name be taken away from his clan because he didn't have a son? Give us property among our father's brothers."*
>
> *Moses brought their case before the Lord. The Lord said to Moses: Zelophehad's daughters are right in what they are saying. By all means, give them property as an inheritance among their father's brothers. Hand over their father's inheritance to them.*
>
> **Numbers 27:1-7 (CEB)**

Many of the stories of women in Scripture are skipped over, particularly when they come near to the larger story of a large heroic character. In the Hebrew Bible, in the Book of Numbers (Chapter 27:1-7), the story of "Zelophehad's daughters," as they are most often referred to, is one of those short narratives you may have missed or skimmed through quickly.

Before we get to their story, though, I want to share how I was keenly reminded of the power of story—real people's stories—on a recent hurricane recovery mission team in Western North Carolina.

As our mission team of sixteen worked in and around the small towns near Asheville, North Carolina, where the devastation of Hurricane Helene continues to impact many people's lives, I heard stories of faith and resilience—stories of gratitude, of appreciating what one has, even when it's very modest by U.S. standards. I heard stories of seeing God at work amid great loss, ongoing poverty, and even death.

During our work, we shared stories back and forth each day as we encountered powerful accounts from the locals. Most mission teams do this. What I noticed was that sometimes the stories that I had shared were later repeated back to me by others, having deeply touched their hearts. We lost track of who had heard which story first. It didn't really matter, because it was the stories that had power—power to touch our hearts and activate compassion, empathy, and even faith within us.

One of those stories that I shared first with our team was repeated back to me by day's end. It was about how I looked into the eyes of a young mom of six children ranging in age from one to nine. I shared that she told me about their survival last winter, having been displaced both during and then again after the storm's flood. She and her family, including a two-month-old, ended up living in a storage shed, trying to keep warm through what she described as life "like settlement times in Appalachia."

In her story, I heard her faith intermingled with the reality of unbelievable challenges and a thankfulness for God's presence and the goodness of people. She said that representatives from Floris United Methodist Church (my church) working there, and others like us, had inspired them to keep their faith and keep going, knowing that God was at work in their lives.

Even so, this mother shared that they were so cold last winter in that storage shed that she thought the baby would die. Yet, on the day she told me this, the child was walking around their camper home, where eight of them currently live. As we finished winterizing their camper on the campus of a United Methodist church, where they were being allowed to shelter now (more than one year after the hurricane), the toddler was filled with hope and energy as I watched her play. Remarkably, the parents seemed to share an unbelievable hope, even though they are still trying to put their lives back together following an unthinkable disaster and hardship.

Her story, and the stories of others we encountered whose lives have been devasted by Helene, continue to shape me—especially when I think my day is hard, when life presents challenges, when I feel the church is too focused on something that doesn't really matter, or even when I feel that our country is off course.

Being immersed in their stories gave me and our whole mission team perspective. A resilient faith that trusts God's guidance, even amid deep hardships, is truly a gift. The stories of such faith can humble us, particularly those of us who sit in seats of privilege. Such stories have the power to inspire us and change us for the better.

We encounter this same kind of resilient faith in Scripture, including in the story of five young women known as the daughters of Zelophehad from the Book of Numbers **(Chapter 27)**. Scripture tells us their names are Mahlah, Noah, Hoglah, Milcah, and Tirzah. I'm guessing these are names you do not know, but we should hear them today (perhaps read them aloud now). In Hebrew, each has an interesting meaning, just as their story does.

The name *Mahlah* means "to move" and "to dance." Noah means "to be in motion" (her name is different from the masculine Noah of the Old Testament, which means "to rest"). Hoglah means "to circle." Milcah means "to walk," and Tirzah means "to run."

As you probably noticed, all the daughters' names have something to do with the concept of "moving" naturally. Yet in Hebrew, these verbs also connote initiative or activity, and that is precisely what these women symbolize as we look at their story and their faith in depth.

Just before Moses dies in Scripture, these women—Mahlah, Noah, Hoglah, Milcah, and Tirzah from the clan of Manasseh, son of Joseph—come before Moses, Eleazar the priest, the chiefs, and the entire community at the entrance of the meeting tent.

The "Tent of Meeting" in Moses' time was the portable sanctuary that the Israelites used during their forty years of wandering in the wilderness. It was the place to meet with God and gather as a community connected in faith and tradition.

The Tent essentially served as a mobile temple—a designated space outside the main camp—where God's presence dwelt and where Moses met and conversed with God. The people also used it for worship and prayer.

The five women come to Moses (and all who are gathered there), explaining that their father died in the wilderness and asking why, since he had no sons, they—as his only adult children—should be forced to give up their inheritance of land in the Promised Land. They ask Moses to give them property among their father's brothers, just as if they were men in the land.

Now, this request may not seem like a big deal today, but in their day, it was against the Law. The existing inheritance custom assumed land passed only through male heirs—sons and then other male agnates—so daughters were excluded from the normal line of succession for such inheritance. This male-only pattern is what "stood on record" as law given to Moses by God, and is what the daughters challenge. The women's challenge to heirship also went against every cultural norm. They lived in a time when women's voices were not heard and often were not valued. They were expected to be silent and find their place (behind men in succession). Therefore, these women certainly knew what it was like not to be seen or valued and to be considered mere property by the male-dominant culture around them.

However, in surprising grace and wisdom, the older Moses takes their case before God. As Numbers recounts their story, God immediately tells Moses: "By all means, give them property as an inheritance among their father's brothers. Hand over their father's inheritance to them" (Numbers 27:7, CEB).

Interestingly, and maybe surprisingly, God in God's

grace makes a way for change here. In effect, God says, "Don't hold anything back—by all means, make this right." God sees that the Law given did not uphold justice for their situation, so God commands Moses to change the Law for such circumstances. The Law may have been written somewhere in stone, but God shows us here that God is willing to change and adapt things to bring forth what is right and just. Verse 7 even says that God says to Moses, "They are right."

These women, whose names speak of lives in motion, do not stand paralyzed in the face of an unjust circumstance. No! They move to initiate change and advocate for themselves, and that courageous act becomes a change written in Scripture for future generations to refer to and learn from.

In studying this text, I learned, interestingly, that the women's actions in this situation have been cited in Supreme Court cases and written into law journals. The precedent of their actions, advocating for themselves when the governing precept is unjust, continues to even shape modern law. Referring to these five sisters and what they teach us, Lauren Wright Pittman writes, "When the powers in place don't budge, that is not the end of the story."[1] Mahlah, Noah, Hoglah, Milcah, and Tirzah show us that God hears us when we are in the right. They also demonstrate that God has the power to change the story, to right wrongs of injustice—even when the wrongs are codified by the powerful (in their day, the men).

Interestingly, it takes a man—Moses—to hear them, even

---

1 Lauren Wright Pittman, *They Stood (Daughters of Zelophehad)*, artist's statement, A Sanctified Art, 2018, https://sanctifiedart.org.

when he perhaps could not see a different way of doing things until God speaks and changes the story. We learn here that God's intervention can make unlikely allies.

When we look at the heart of God revealed in the Bible, we see a God of justice for all people, a God who seeks to include and offer fairness, even when that requires change in systems, the Law itself, and the way things have always been done. This heart of God revealed is where we see an intersection of faith and Law, and yes, even faith and politics, when it comes to the story of the oppressed.

Writing about the intersection of these areas of faith, justice, and politics in South Africa, Archbishop Desmond Tutu questioned, "Would you say Moses was a religious leader or a political leader? Was God acting religiously or politically when He set free a slave people?"[2]

Sometimes, in our faith in a God of justice, we, like these Hebrew sisters in Numbers, must move to advocate for what is right in the places of power. Moses did this despite Pharaoh's oppression. His story is linked to the story of these women. The sisters come as those oppressed in the land. The one formerly oppressed is approached by the oppressed. You see, our stories sometimes connect with others when we are willing to look with depth at our common journeys.

These women teach us that we can be a part of change that impacts us and those who come after us. Against the odds, they courageously show us that the story can be changed, no matter how long injustice has been codified!

We also learn from this text that when injustice does not

---

[2] Desmond Tutu, *God Has a Dream: A Vision of Hope for Our Time* (New York: Doubleday, 2005).

impact us, as in Moses' case in this narrative, we still need to evaluate such situations through God's vision of inclusion and expansive grace. With that insight, then we are to do what we can to bring about change in flawed and oppressive situations and systems. This story teaches us that we must care about other people's stories, too!

Beyond this, as we read about Moses, it is striking that this was one of his last actions in the eyes of God's people. Remember, everyone was gathered at the Tent. He granted these women inclusion and justice (who would have otherwise become dependents at best) as one of his last actions as leader of God's people. Moses is signaling a change in the works as God comes in closer to those who are oppressed.

What can we learn here from this story?

Again, this could be read simply as a good story—one we may have skipped over in Scripture in past studies—but reading it now reveals something new. I believe the learning here invites us to go deeper still. The story of these five women—whose names signify some sort of movement—can speak to us about where God is calling us to get up and get moving, walking, dancing, running, or encircling so that God's justice and ways of grace might be shared.

As the Spirit moves us now, where does the story of someone or some group need an infusion of change, justice, freedom, or hope?

It is no accident that when Jesus gave us the Great Commission in our New Testament, he gave it as an action. Jesus said, "Go therefore and make disciples of all nations, baptizing them in the name of the Father and of the Son and of the Holy Spirit and teaching them to obey everything that I have commanded you. And remember, I am with you always, to the end of the age" (Matthew 28:19-20, CEB). We are to go, make, baptize, and teach the ways of Jesus, knowing he is with us in this work.

Our faith is operative. The calling of Christ is to action. So, your faith—our shared faith—is meant to be in courageous motion, even when it moves against the odds!

Have you ever thought about what your life might be like if people had not stepped forward to make change—to change stories, listen well, and advocate for what is right and good? What about all the Moses types in your story that, when encountering the hard moments of others, go to God and share their hearts? What about the ones who hear the stories, and in turn, truly listen for God's guidance, like Moses did when presented with the sisters' request?

Have you thought about the ones before you who stepped up and said, I've prayed about this, and we need to make a change! We need to make a way. We must support the rights of these people! Consider the brave ancestors of your faith who stood their ground and said on behalf of others: Their stories must be different because justice is needed, and I (we) can help that happen!

I was struck recently by an interview with Jane Goodall on *The Project*[3] produced with the intention that it not be shown until after her death. The premise was that it would be her final words to the world. The result was profound, to say the least, and, in my opinion, very much worth watching.

---

3 *Famous Last Words: Jane Goodall,* documentary film, directed by Brad Falchuk, distributed by Netflix, 2025, https://youtube.com/shorts/f2KgGR9hoj8?si=ncC1jh0CS3jeg4Vg.

Here is some of Jane's final wisdom on what it means to live a life of hope and in action. I quote:

- "I was somebody sent to this world to try to give people hope in dark times, because without hope, we fall into apathy and do nothing."
- "Even if this is the end of humanity as we know it, let's fight to the very end."
- "Each and every one of you has a role to play. You may not know it, you may not find it, but your life matters and you are here for a reason."
- "What you do makes a difference, and you have to decide what kind of difference you want to make."

Goodall's words speak to knowing that life—your life—has purpose. She shares with clarity that there are choices that require action and impact change. Her story—her life—was filled with so much of that kind of purposeful, hope-filled action right up to her very last days, as she advocated for animals, people, and our precious planet. Her example for our generation and for generations to come stands tall, much like the story of the sisters Mahlah, Noah, Hoglah, Milcah, and Tirzah. With their story in mind, we are challenged to consider where we are being called to make a difference—large or small—that just might positively impact future generations.

Friends, I hope you learn from the story of Mahlah, Noah, Hoglah, Milcah, and Tirzah that sometimes you must move. Your calling in the faith requires courageous action(s). That action—the holy movement toward an outcome different from the way things are or have always been—sometimes also requires you to use your voice to speak for justice and advocate against prevailing norms, making a vital difference. When you move, act, and speak for justice, even when you think you may not be valued, God hears and, in turn, values you and your story, no matter how you got to where you are.

With a beloved sense of value, like that affirmed by God in Mahlah, Noah, Hoglah, Milcah, and Tirzah, the Spirit of God can bring about the winds of change in the circumstances of your life and in the world around you, changing the story and the outcome. This movement can bring unexpected allies, like Moses to the five sisters, and often gives birth to hope and even radical transformation.

As you know these sisters now and their brave example, I hope their influence helps you see the potential for a new story to unfold in your life. Where is God calling you to move, to speak, to bring change for the good, and to change the story of someone or something? You can sit on that calling. You can say within yourself that there's no hope and even argue that your actions or voice do not matter in the large picture of a complex world. You might have a long history of excuses to avoid stepping up, stating, even more simply, that you do not have the time or energy to get involved. Too often, our excuses and fears hinder God's work through us. Yet, like the five sisters in Numbers, we are called to step forward to help change the story. It takes a different impulse to move in this direction, and it takes faith to move past our excuses and fears toward the powerful movement of God's grace.

Your courage to step into God's story can transform what seems unchangeable, even when the odds appear stacked against you. The witness of Scripture reminds us, again and again, that God's Spirit moves through the most unlikely people to bring holy and just change. You may be the very instrument God uses to ensure those who are ignored are finally heard, and those who are unseen are finally known, especially in a world that prefers to silence cries for justice. So, as you hear the cry of the needy, may you dare to be bold, let the stories of others shape you, and join God in changing what is hard to change in our world today.

Prayer:

God, we so appreciate that you are a God who surprises us. Even when things seem hard-fixed and locked down, you have a miraculous way of seeing us and hearing us, and then nudging us forward in the way of grace, opening windows and doors and moving us steadily toward being perfected in you. For the times we have sat too quietly in our hardships or looked apathetically past the hardships of others, forgive us, we pray. Join our story intimately with yours. Free us now to move with the might of your justice rolling forward like great waters in dry lands. We pray in the powerful and holy name of Jesus Christ. Amen!

Reflection Questions:

1. Are you willing to impact "the story" by moving faithfully into new possibilities that God desires for you and perhaps others?

2. Where is God calling you to move, speak, or bring change for the good—to change the story of someone or something?

3. Who are some potential allies for you as you seek to act in the way of justice with God?

4. How do the last words of Jane Goodall—"What you do makes a difference, and you have to decide what kind of difference you want to make"—speak to a life lived faithfully to God?

About the Writer:

Gina Anderson-Cloud is the lead pastor of Floris United Methodist Church, a large membership congregation in Herndon, Virginia. Passionate about bridging the church to the world, Gina has fruitfully led large and mid-size churches for more than 25 years, and before ministry served in community social work as an advocate for those on the margins.

CHAPTER FIVE

Rahab: An Uncommon Call

By Dr. Aleze M. Fulbright

Scripture Lesson: Joshua 2:1-24; Joshua 6:20-25

> *Joshua let Rahab the prostitute live, her family, and everyone related to her. So her family still lives among Israel today, because she hid the spies whom Joshua had sent to scout out Jericho."*
>
> **Joshua 6:25 (CEB)**

Understanding the Call

"One's call should not be mistaken for one's job. A call is bigger than what we do for a living. It defines God's intentions for our lives."[4]

Growing up, my understanding of those who were "called by God" was shaped by an image of spiritual perfection: individuals who seemed to live flawless lives, crowned with unwavering holiness and certainty. In my imagination, those who were called appeared almost untouched by struggle or moral complexity. However, as I matured in faith and ministry and studied the stories of Scripture more deeply, I discovered something far more profound. The faithful giants of the Bible and even many of my real-life (s)heroes were not perfect people. Rather, they were individuals marked by unwavering faith, courageous obedience, and hearts surrendered to God's leading.

---

[4] Melissa Lauber, "God's Call," *Ministry Matters*, December 27, 2011, https://ministrymatters.com/2011-12-27_god_s_call/.

Perhaps that is why I am continually surprised that the biblical character of Rahab is not more prominently lifted up when we speak about responding to God's call. For me, Rahab provides one of the most powerful examples of humility, courage, and responsiveness to God's invitation to participate in the expansion of God's Kin-dom.

Understanding Rahab's Call

> *Joshua, Nun's son, secretly sent two men as spies from Shittim. He said, "Go. Look over the land, especially Jericho. They set out and entered the house of a prostitute named Rahab. They bedded down there."*
>
> **Joshua 2:1 (CEB)**

Rahab is, in many ways, the most unexpected character in the biblical narrative. She is a Canaanite woman living within a city that stands in opposition to Israel. Yet at a critical moment in Israel's journey, Rahab collaborates with God's people in a way that ultimately saves not only the spies she shelters, but also herself and her entire family.

Scripture introduces Rahab as a prostitute, though scholars have long debated the fuller nature of her profession. Some suggest that Rahab may have operated an inn or guesthouse built into the wall of Jericho, a strategic location for weary travelers entering the city. Others argue that she may have served as a temple prostitute, which in Canaanite culture was not viewed with the same moral condemnation as in Israelite society.[5] Still other scholars note that prostitution in the ancient world often emerged from economic desperation. Women without social protection, marriage prospects, or family resources sometimes turned

---

5 Marion Ann Taylor and Christiana de Groot, eds., *Women of War, Women of Woe: Joshua and Judges through the Eyes of Nineteenth-Century Female Biblical Interpreters* (Grand Rapids, MI: William Eerdmans Publishing Company, 2016).

to such work simply to survive and to provide for their families.[6] Whatever the precise circumstances of her life, Rahab emerges as an independent businesswoman navigating complex realities within her society.

Rahab would seem to be the most unlikely person for God to call into partnership with the divine mission. She is a woman, a foreigner, and someone whose profession carried significant stigma. And yet, when the moment arrives, Rahab demonstrates a faith that is not merely spoken but lived. Her response to God's progressing work can be understood through three defining characteristics: the three Rs of Rahab's calling:

1. Risk-Taking Mission and Service

> *But the woman had taken the two men and hidden them. Then she said, "Of course the men came to me. But I didn't know where they were from."*
>
> **Joshua 2:4 (CEB)**

Rahab knowingly risks her own life to protect the Israelite spies. In doing so, she defies the authority of her own city and places herself in grave danger. Her actions are not passive or accidental; they are deliberate. Rahab recognizes that something greater than political allegiance is unfolding. She is willing to place her safety, livelihood, and future on the line for the sake of God's purposes, understanding that true calling often requires this kind of courage and the willingness to act even when the outcome is uncertain.

2. Radical Hospitality

> *But she had taken them up to the roof and hidden them under the flax stalks that she had laid out on the roof.*
>
> **Joshua 2:6 (CEB)**

---

[6] Irene Nowell, *Women in the Old Testament* (Collegeville, MN: Liturgical Press, 1997).

Hospitality is a recurring theme throughout Scripture, and Rahab embodies it in a radical way. She not only welcomes the spies but actively protects them, using her own home as a place of refuge. Her hospitality is more than kindness; it is strategic compassion. Rahab recognizes the moment and responds decisively. Her home becomes sacred ground where God's larger story is quietly unfolding.

3. Relentless Faith in God

> *I know that the Lord has given you the land. Terror over you has overwhelmed us. The entire population of the land has melted down in fear because of you. We have heard how the Lord dried up the water of the Reed Sea in front of you when you left Egypt. We have also heard what you did to Sihon and Og, the two kings of the Amorites on the other side of the Jordan. You utterly wiped them out. We heard this and our hearts turned to water. Because of you, people can no longer work up their courage. This is because the Lord your God is God in heaven above and on earth below.*
>
> **Joshua 2:9-11 (CEB)**

Perhaps the most remarkable aspect of Rahab's story is her theological clarity. Though she is not an Israelite, she recognizes the sovereignty of Israel's God. She recounts the stories she has heard, from the crossing of the Red Sea and Israel's victories over enemy kings and interprets them as evidence that God is actively moving in history. Rahab's confession of faith is one of the most striking declarations found in the Book of Joshua. Her faith is not inherited tradition; it is discernment born of observation and courage.

Transformed by God's call, Rahab's faith, courage,

and concern for others saved her family and herself. Rahab was brave, decisive, and quick to give orders. Rahab is an inspiration, as she experienced conversion from harlot to heroine. In addition, there are scriptural references that call Rahab worthy, listing her by name in the hallmark of faith (Hebrews 11:31). Because of Rahab's faith, God saved Rahab in every sense of the word. Rahab gave birth to a son, Boaz, who married a woman named Ruth, the great-grandmother of King David. Ultimately, Rahab is listed in the first chapter of Matthew's Gospel as part of the lineage of Jesus.

As Lynn Japinga observes, "Maybe the name prostitute does not matter so much to God. The authors emphasized her sinfulness, but perhaps God saw a woman who did what she had to do to save herself and her family. God saw the courageous choices she made to help the spies. In God's vocabulary, maybe her name was not Rahab the prostitute, but Rahab the faithful, Rahab the courageous, Rahab the quick-thinking negotiator, or Rahab the wise."[7]

Understanding Our Response

"The call" is often equated with pulpit ministry or becoming a missionary overseas, when in fact the varying expressions of God's call can be lived out by God's grace through everyday means of service and by people of varying types. The celebration to the call of uncommon people is the willing response to utilize our God-given gifts and graces, skills and abilities, and resources to manifest the Gospel Message.

---

[7] Lynn Japinga, *Preaching the Women of the Old Testament: Who They Were and Why They Matter* (Louisville, KY: Westminster John Knox Press, 2017).

As stated earlier, "*One's call should not be mistaken for one's job. A call is bigger than what we do for a living. It defines God's intentions for our lives.*" When reading about this faithful woman, she is often referred as "Rahab the prostitute," but the negative label and the actions of her past did not determine her destiny. Rahab's example demonstrates a living faith in a forgiving and grace-filled God. Without a doubt, Rahab helped to save the lives of the Israelite spies, which in turn set Israel on the path toward the Promised Land.

Rahab's witness challenges us to reconsider how quickly we determine who God can or cannot use for God's greater purposes. May we not confine God, or those whom God calls, to our societal boxes that contain our comforts and expectations. May we learn to see the holy potential in all people. And may we remember that God can mend the broken pieces of our lives, to become a transformational witness of God's great care and unconditional love.

Reflection Questions

1. Rahab risked everything to live in and out of her calling. What risks are you willing to take for the sake of God's calling?

2. Whether Rahab was an innkeeper or a harlot, her life demonstrates that God calls people from unexpected places. How does Rahab's story challenge our assumptions about who God can use?

3. Responding to the call requires faith, as evidenced by Rahab's witness, at what point do we allow our faith to overtake our fears as we respond to God's call?

4. Too often, we judge a person's future by their past. How do we sometimes limit or dismiss someone's calling potential because of their previous behaviors or life circumstances?

About the Writer:

Dr. Aleze M. Fulbright is an ordained elder in The United Methodist Church who is a person of conviction in living a personal mission to encourage, equip, and empower all people to live with purpose and live out their God-givenness.

CHAPTER SIX

Deborah

A One-of-a-Kind Leader

By Bishop Debra Wallace-Padgett

Scripture Lesson: Judges, Chapters 4 and 5

When you hear the phrase "one of a kind," what comes to your mind?

Snowflakes? After all, technically, every snowflake is unique. Created when a waterdrop freezes on a particle in the sky, the snowflake keeps changing as it moves through varying temperatures while falling to the earth. Even though it is estimated that planet Earth receives a septillion snowflakes annually, each is "one of a kind" because, as they pass through different temperatures and humidities, they develop unique shapes and sizes.[8]

How about experiences that happen at church? One-of-a-kind "church" stories abound in my family. Some are funny, others tragic, all unique. I am sure many of you have these types of stories in your memory bank, too!

Then there are some amazing one-of-a-kind athletes. Tom Brady, Simone Biles, Alysa Liu, Caitlyn Clark, and Shohei Ohtani are a sampling of athletes with extraordinary skills and achievements.

---

[8] Library of Congress, "Is It True That No Two Snow Crystals Are Alike?" *Everyday Mysteries*, accessed February 21, 2026, https://www.loc.gov/everyday-mysteries/meteorology-climatology/item/is-it-true-that-no-two-snow-crystals-are-alike/.

What about amazing one-of-a-kind leaders? Our Scripture passage describes such a leader. Her name is Deborah, and she is a one-of-a-kind leader of the very best variety.

There is much to admire about Deborah. First, consider her name. I do not say this just because my mom had the biblical "shero" in mind when naming me. (Mom has told me that her only regret about my name is that she spelled it "Debra" instead of the biblical rendition of "Deborah." I have replied that I love the spelling she chose.

A name communicates much about a person—at least that is what a leader of a church I once served seemed to think. I do not know if this is still the case in Kentucky, but at that time, when a pastoral change occurred, the district superintendent convened a covenant meeting between the Staff-Parish Relations Committee of the receiving church and the newly appointed pastor. This get-acquainted meeting in which the district superintendent introduced the Staff-Parish Relations Committee and me to each other seemed to go well. As we mingled at the conclusion of the meeting, though, one of the leaders pulled me to the side, saying, "Your name is Debra Wallace-Padgett?" I replied, "Yes, the Wallace-Padgett is hyphenated." He responded, "Well, that will take some getting used to!" I thought, but did not say aloud, "*You* are going to take some getting used to! (This is what a colleague of mine calls *keeping your head voice inside.)*

Just as my last name apparently communicated a great deal about me to the church leader (who, by the way, quickly adapted to my hyphenated name, supporting me in splendid ways), the name of the Deborah in Judges 4 and 5 communicates much about her. Deborah, in Hebrew, means "bee" and is associated with adjectives like industrious, wise, and practical—all qualities desirable for effective judges.

Though not the only Deborah in the Bible (think Rebekah's nurse in Genesis 35:8), she is the sole one who is also a judge. In fact, she is the only female judge in all of Hebrew Scriptures. The Book of Judges lists twelve judges by name. 1 Samuel adds Samuel, Eli, and his sons, and 1 Chronicles names Kenaniah and his sons. But there is one woman judge, and her name is Deborah.

Deborah lives up to her good name by offering *sound* judgment and *wise* counsel to the people of Israel. Indeed, Judges 4 paints a picture of a judge so effective that the palm tree under which she sits while working is named in her honor.

> *At that time Deborah, a prophetess, wife of Lappidoth, was judging Israel. She used to sit under the palm of Deborah between Ramah and Bethel in the hill country of Ephraim; and the Israelites came up to her for judgment.*
>
> **Judges 4:4-5 (NRSVue)**

Imagine with me this one-of-a-kind leader fulfilling her work as a judge while sitting under a palm tree that bears her name. She is as busy as a bee, helping people sort through the challenges and problems in their personal lives and community. She lives up to her name with wise counsel, industrious spirit, and practical advice.

Some people embody their birth name or nickname. For others, a different word captures who they are in Christ. How are you living up to your name or a different word that describes you?

There is more to admire about Deborah than her name, though. In addition, her military leadership style is exemplary. The judges in her day did more than arbitrate disagreements between people. On occasion, they were also tasked with leading the military in solo, heroic ways. Examples include Samson, Gideon, and Jephthah.

Not Deborah. She is a leader who empowers.

I offer a confession to you. The killing and conquests described in passages like Judges 4 and 5 make me very uncomfortable.

Judges 5:28-30 *Song of Deborah* is a case in point.

Out of the window she peered,
the mother of Sisera gazed through the lattice:
"Why is his chariot so long in coming?
Why tarry the hoofbeats of his chariots?"
Her wisest ladies make answer,
indeed, she answers the question herself:
Are they not finding and dividing the spoil?—
A girl or two for every man;
spoil of dyed stuffs for Sisera,
spoil of dyed stuffs embroidered,
two pieces of dyed work embroidered for my neck as spoil?"

Judges 5:28-30 (NRSVue)

General Sisera's mother expects that once the Israelis are conquered, their material possessions will be taken. Worse, their young girls will be raped and treated in inhumane ways, one or two for every man. The content in this passage of Scripture is horrifying!

Also, General Sisera's mother is looking forward to the safe return of her decorated hero son (who we know is dead). She asks, "Why is his chariot so long in coming?

Why tarry the hoofbeats of his chariots?" (Judges 5:28b, NRSVue). This scene tugs at the hearts of mothers across all nations and generations.

Yes, I typically avoid preaching and teaching from war texts because of the cringe factor and my inability to fully reconcile them theologically. With that acknowledgement, let us delve into Deborah's capacity as a leader to empower. She is a military leader who shares the limelight and power.

Chapter 4 starts with the familiar up-and-down pattern for the period of the judges. The people would follow God under a faithful judge until that judge died. Then they would lose their way under a different leader. Another faithful judge would rise to leadership, and the people of Israel would turn back to God. Then, after that judge's death, they would fall away from God again.

"The Israelites again did what was evil in the sight of the Lord, after Ehud died" (Judges 4:1, NRSVue). They are conquered by King Jabin of Canaan, who, with the help of General Sisera, oppresses them for twenty years. Deborah, who is both a prophetess and judge, sends for Barak to defeat Sisera and his army. Barak's response is surprising:

> *Barak said to her, "If you will go with me, I will go; but if you will not go with me, I will not go."*
>
> **Judges 4:8 (NRSVue)**

The text does not specify Barak's motivation for his conditional agreement. Is it an affront to Deborah's authority? A taunt? A demonstration of respect for her abilities?

Though we do not know Barak's reason for the response, we are clear on Deborah's answer: Sure, I'll go with you. Know this, though. The glory will go to a woman!

And she said, "I will surely go with you; nevertheless, the road on which you are going will not lead to your glory, for the Lord will sell Sisera into the hand of a woman."

Judges 4:9a (NRSVue)

Deborah accompanies Barak on the mission to which he is called. They gather 10,000 troops from the tribes of Naphtali and Zebulun to convene on Mt. Tabor. General Sisera responds by assembling his army, including 900 chariots. Then at the right moment, Deborah deploys Barak and his troops into battle (Judges 4:9-16).

Barak is not the only person to experience Deborah's empowering leadership. When she tells Barak, "... the Lord will sell Sisera into the hand of a woman" (Judges 4:9, NRSVue), Deborah is not referencing herself. The catalyst for Sisera's death is a Kenite woman. The Kenites trace their heritage through Moses' father-in-law Jethro, possibly to Cain. The Kenite clan is thought to have eventually assimilated into the tribe of Judah.

Here is what happens in this segment of the narrative. The Canaanite general, Sisera, flees for his life after the Israelites decimate his army. He happens upon Jael, who is coming out to meet him. Knowing that Jael is the wife of Heber the Kenite, whose tribe is at peace with King Jabor of Canaan, Sisera accepts the invitation to enter her tent. He requests water to quench his thirst and also asks Jael to hide him from the enemy under a rug in the tent. She does so, after giving him milk (presumably to make him sleepy). Once he is asleep, she hammers a tent peg into his temple.

In Deborah's Song, the people of Israel praise Jael's actions as heroic under desperate circumstances.

Most blessed of women be Jael,
the wife of Heber the Kenite,
of tent-dwelling women most blessed.

Judges 5:24 (NRSVue)

Deborah empowers Jael by highlighting her important role in the victory. By including Jael in her song, the spotlight is not confined to Deborah and Barak. Instead, she opens the door for another courageous woman to share the "glory."

You and I have numerous opportunities to empower others to fulfill their leadership potential. Our empowerment may occur through conversations, walking with someone through a difficult leadership task, or publicly affirming a leader who is demonstrating remarkable courage and creativity. Empowering leaders opens doors for others to fulfill their one-of-a-kind roles.

Deborah's life inspires these questions: Who are you empowering currently? Who will you intentionally empower in the future?

Deborah is a one-of-a-kind leader, as demonstrated by her name and propensity to empower others. And still, there is more. She had an extraordinary capacity to balance and hold many roles.

I have a set of John Wesley's journals, which help me know more about the thought processes and theology of the father of Methodism. I wish we had Deborah's journals. Oh my, the stories they would tell. Perhaps they would describe some of the most "unique" cases she negotiated, what she thought about Barak's request for her to go with him into battle, the holy habits she practiced, her husband's cooking abilities, the pain she experienced as a result of being a barrier-breaker, the disappointments in her life, her greatest joys, and more.

The closest thing we have to a journal from Deborah is found in Judges Chapters 4 and 5. Her life story is presented in two forms: narrative (Chapter 4) and poetry (Chapter 5).

In reading these two chapters, we quickly realize that this woman knows how to multitask with grace! She is a prophetess, a wife, a judge, a military leader, a songwriter, and a singer. If that isn't enough, she is called the "mother of Israel" (Judges 5:7b, NRSVue)! And she does all of this while wearing high heels! (Oops—I just transported her into the 21st century.)

What Judges 4 and 5 do not tell us is how she keeps all these plates spinning without dropping one. I suspect we know the answer to that question because every one of us faces a similar challenge. We know that keeping balance in our lives requires prioritizing which plates to spin and which to hand off.

This brings me to a fourth and final question: Are there any plates you need to stop spinning to have the time and energy to be your best self?

Yes, I admire Deborah, a one-of-a-kind leader who lives up to her name. Each of us is one-of-a-kind, too. May we, like Deborah, be known for our one-of-a-kind way of leading and serving. Amen and Amen.

Prayer:

God, thank you for inspiring biblical leaders like Deborah, who fulfilled your design for her life. Help us do the same in our lives and service. Amen.

Reflection Questions:

1. How are you living up to your name or a different word that describes you?

2. Who are you empowering?

3. Who will you intentionally empower in the future?

4. What plates do you need to stop spinning in order to have the time and energy to be your best self?

About the Writer:

Bishop Debra Wallace-Padgett serves two conferences in two jurisdictions: Holston Conference, Southeastern Jurisdiction and West Virginia Conference, Northeastern Jurisdiction. In August, 2024, Bishop Wallace-Padgett was elected as the president of the World Methodist Council.

CHAPTER SEVEN

The Story of Ruth

A Plea for Tolerance

By Stella Roberts

Scripture Lesson: Ruth 4:13-17

> *So Boaz took Ruth and she became his wife. When they came together, the Lord made her conceive, and she bore a son. Then the women said to Naomi, "Blessed be the Lord, who has not left you this day without next-of-kin; and may his name be renowned in Israel. He shall be to you a restorer of life and a nourisher of your old age; for your daughter-in-law who loves you, who is more to you than seven sons, has borne him. Then Naomi took the child and laid him in her bosom, and she became his nurse. The women of the neighborhood gave him a name, saying, "A son has been born to Naomi." They named him Obed; he was the father of Jesse, the father of David.*
>
> **Ruth 4:3-17 (NRSVue)**

The story of Ruth is probably familiar to most of us as a story about the loving relationship between a woman and her daughter-in-law. However, its importance goes far beyond being a love story. If we can understand how the Book of Ruth fits into the Hebrew Scriptures as a whole and why Ruth's story is included in the biblical canon, we can learn that it has something important to say to us today.

The two main characters in the story are Naomi, a Jew, and Ruth, her Moabite daughter-in-law. At this period of their history, the Israelites generally considered the Moabites to be despised enemies. Moab would certainly not be a place Jews would choose to go under normal circumstances. But there is famine in Bethlehem, known as the "land of bread" (kind of ironic to have a famine in "the land of bread"), so Naomi, her husband, Elimelech, their two sons, and presumably many other Israelites, travel to Moab in search of food. The names of the two sons should give us a clue that there might be trouble ahead. One is named Mahlon (which means "sickness and death"), and the other is named Chilion (which means "annihilation").

Despite all that, they do find food in Moab, and they also find that the Moabites aren't such bad people after all. They are generous, sharing their food with the Israelites and eventually even intermarrying with them—it's nice to know there is at least one biblical precedent that demonstrates ancient enemies can, indeed, live in peace together. The family is not in Moab long, however, before Naomi's husband, Elimelech, dies, leaving Naomi with her two sons (the ones with the distressing names). Both of the sons marry Moabite women—Orpah and Ruth, and they settle there for about ten years until both the sons die, leaving three women as widows, without men to care for them (which made them very vulnerable in that day and time).

Naomi decides that her best option is to return to Judah to live with her family. The famine in Judah had ended by this time, and there was plenty of food in "the land of bread," so Naomi urged her daughters-in-law to return to their families in Moab. One daughter-in-law, Orpah, does leave, but Ruth does not. She instead responds with these famous words:

Do not press me to leave you or to turn back from your company, for wherever you go, I will go, and wherever you live, I will live. Your people shall be my people, and your God, my God. Wherever you die, I will die and there I will be buried. May the Lord do this thing to me and more also, if even death should come between us!

Ruth 1:16-17 (NRSVue)

Ruth accompanies Naomi home to Judah, journeying specifically to Bethlehem, the home of Naomi's deceased husband, Elimelech. There, they encounter a relative of Elimelech—a wealthy man named Boaz. They glean in Boaz's barley fields, as was customary for widows to do, gathering what the reapers have left behind. And the reapers intentionally leave some behind so others might be fed. Boaz notices Ruth and takes a liking to her. He sees that the fields in which she gleans are especially fruitful; he cautions his men against molesting her, and he allows her access to his employees' water supply. At mealtime, he offers her food. This is indeed special treatment for this Moabite woman.

Naomi, recognizing Boaz's kindness as affection for Ruth and recognizing the need for a more permanent solution for Ruth's future than seasonal gleaning, then plays matchmaker. Says Naomi:

"My daughter, I need to seek a home for you, so that it may be well with you. Now here is our kinsman Boaz, with whose young women you have been working. See, he is winnowing barley tonight at the threshing floor. Now wash and anoint yourself, and put on your best clothes and go down to the threshing floor; but do not make yourself known to the man until he has finished eating and drinking. When he lies down, observe the place where he lies; then, go, and uncover his feet and lie down; and he will tell you what to do." And she replied, "All that you tell me I will do."

Ruth 3:1-5 (NRSVue)

Naomi's directive to Ruth to "uncover his feet and lie down" has strong sexual overtones. Naomi is telling Ruth to engage in risky behavior that would carry a high potential for scandal: to go to a place where she does not belong in the middle of the night to proposition a man who is her social superior. Despite the risk, Ruth does just as Naomi instructs her. When Boaz wakes and finds Ruth lying at his feet, he says:

> *"Who are you?" And she answered, "I am Ruth, your servant; spread your skirt over your servant, for you are next-of-kin." And he said, "May you be blessed by the Lord, my daughter; this last instance of your loyalty is better than the first; you have not gone after young men, whether poor or rich. And now, my daughter, do not be afraid, I will do for you all that you ask."*
>
> **Ruth 3:9-11 (NRSVue)**

The upshot of this tryst is that Boaz (the Israelite) and Ruth (the Moabite) are eventually married. Boaz, in fact, purchases Ruth and all of Elimelech's property from Naomi and, at the time of purchase, announces his intention to marry Ruth. Then comes the climax of this whole story:

> *So Boaz took Ruth and she became his wife. When they came together, the Lord made her conceive, and she bore a son. Then the women said to Naomi, "Blessed be the Lord, who has not left you this day without next of kin; and may his name be renowned in Israel! He shall be to you a restorer of life and a nourisher of your old age; for your daughter-in-law who loves you who is more to you than seven sons, has borne him." Then Naomi took the child and laid him in her bosom, and became his nurse. And the women of the neighborhood gave him a name, saying, "A son has been born to Naomi." They named him Obed; he was the father of Jesse, the father of David.*
>
> **Ruth 4:13-17 (NRSVue)**

End of Story

This beautiful story is about a loving relationship between a woman and her daughter-in-law, which ends happily ever after. It is, however, not truly religious in the traditional sense of that term. Aside from Ruth's conversion to Judaism, there is no deep or hidden revelation about God here. There is precious little about the human relationship to God. And there is no direct reference to how God might be involved in the story. What, then, is it doing in the Hebrew Bible? The key question is, why is the story of Ruth included in the Hebrew Scriptures?

Though Ruth's story is set in that time frame of Israel's history (around 1100 BCE), it is generally accepted by biblical scholars that the tale was not told until centuries later. In fact, it has nothing in common with the historical concerns or the literary style of the judges' period and is dated by scholars as post-exilic—that is, coming from a much later time in Israel's history.

According to many scholars, the Book of Ruth was recorded after the period of the judges, after the monarchy was established, after Saul, David, and Solomon ruled as kings in the united kingdom, after the prophets, after the Babylonian captivity and exile, and after the return of the exiles to Jerusalem. After all this history—about seven hundred years—somebody remembers Ruth! "Why?" is extremely important!

Remember that the period of exile was an incredibly difficult time for the people of Israel. The Promised Land was gone. The Davidic line of kings was gone. The Babylonians had dispersed the people into various communities and subcultures, taking away from them everything Jewish, so they would lose their identities and slowly be absorbed into the culture of their captors. That way, Judaism and its belief in the one God, Yahweh, would be gone forever. Pretty drastic stuff, this, in a hard, hard time.

Then, to maintain the people's identity and faith during the exile, their priests developed the law of God to the nth degree. They held together by following God's law, and, assured by the priests' and prophets' proclamation of a Messiah, they persevered. Times eventually got better because Cyrus of Persia's policy was different. He believed that the way to govern Persia's subject people was to keep them happy. So, rather than wipe out the Hebrews, he let them go home. Under Sheshbazaar's leadership, the Jews gathered their belongings and returned home.

The problem now was that some of their leaders—most notably Ezra (as priest) and Nehemiah (as governor)—still had a kind of siege mentality. They wanted the Jews not only to be identifiable but also to be set apart—even exclusive. They got carried away. Judaism began to draw in upon itself and emphasize pure blood as a necessity.

Ezra and Nehemiah made three demands on the Jews. To be considered an authentic Jew, you had to, one, be loyal to and supportive of the temple; you had to, two, be fully devoted to keeping the law in all its requirements; and three, you had to be of pure Jewish blood. This last point is crucial. Seeking to rid Judaism of foreign influences after the exile, Ezra and Nehemiah forced the returning exiles to cast out foreign wives and the children born of those wives. Only those of pure stock could consider themselves Jews.

Intermarriages were dissolved then and there and are forbidden in the future.

Considering all this, the Book of Ruth relates to and is critical of this restricted and exclusive understanding of Judaism. Following the return of the exiles and around seven hundred years after her death, someone remembers and retells the story of Ruth, the Moabite who lived so many years before. And they did so for a reason!

Hear the end of the story again:

> *So Boaz took Ruth and she became his wife. When they came together, the Lord made her conceive, and she bore a son. Then Naomi took the child and laid him in her bosom, and she became his nurse. And the women of the neighborhood gave him a name, saying, "A son has been born to Naomi." They named him Obed; he was the father of Jesse, the father of David.*
>
> **Ruth 4:13-17 (NRSVue)**

The point, finally, is that in the face of the returned Jews' restrictiveness, intolerance, and exclusivity, someone has the good sense to remember Ruth, mother of Obed, grandmother of Jesse, great-grandmother of David. Someone had the sense to remember Ruth, the MOABITE (the foreigner, the outsider, the immigrant). And in this recollection, the ridiculousness of restricting and making too exclusive the requirements of Judaism is highlighted. If Ezra's and Nehemiah's rules had been in force earlier, David, the great King David, would not have been considered a Jew. That's because David, who was descended from a Moabite great-grandmother, was not of pure blood.

Since the woman, Ruth, was a Moabite, not an Israelite, the book's effect, if not its purpose, is to create a sympathetic feeling toward foreigners and immigrants who are also protected by Israel's God. So, the suggestion here is that the Book of Ruth is a post-exilic composition based on a much older tale intended to counteract the harsh decrees of Ezra and Nehemiah, which required Hebrew men to divorce their foreign wives and marry only within the covenant community. And the book performs that service admirably. How silly it is, the Book of Ruth implies, to be so restrictive, so exclusive, and so intolerant as to deny David his citizenship within Judaism. To Ezra, Nehemiah, and the many in their stead, Ruth says clearly, The love of God is bigger than you know! The love of God is bigger than any of us knows!

Ezra and Nehemiah wanted to limit God's covenant love to include only those like them—those of pure Jewish blood. And the story of Ruth is remembered and recorded to vehemently counteract that limitation!

Today, I fear the temptation is, similarly, to limit the message of God—the message of God's love and grace—to those who look like we do, think as we do, love as we do, and act as we do. Sometimes the divisions are geographical, sometimes racial or ethnic, sometimes political, and sometimes gender-based.

But the message Scripture proclaims to us today is that we should not fall prey to those temptations. Indeed, we must not fall prey to those temptations. Instead, we should, we can, and we do strongly oppose them—oppose any effort to limit God's love. Christ's church has no requirement pertaining to bloodline. You don't have to be a Southerner or even an American to be welcome in Christ's church. You don't have to be a certain color or have attained a particular economic status. You can be male or female. You can be undocumented, an alien, or a dreamer and still be loved by God and of critical importance to God, and thus, loved and of critical importance to those of us who claim to be followers of God incarnate—Jesus Christ.

You see, the story of Ruth is, in reality, a story of tolerance, inclusiveness, and love without limits. And the message of the Book of Ruth in the Hebrew Scriptures is tolerance.

It's important, though, to clarify what "tolerance" means, for that word has received a bad rap among some circles today. Unfortunately, tolerance has been equated with apathy—sitting back in the midst of evil, injustice, discrimination, suffering, and persecution—just accepting all that as "the way things are" and doing little to work for change. That is not at all the message Ruth is conveying. When we look up some dictionary definitions of tolerance, this is what we find:

> *Tolerance is a fair, objective, and permissive attitude toward those whose opinions, beliefs, practices, racial or ethnic origins, etc., differ from one's own; Tolerance is freedom from bigotry.*[9]

This is the kind of tolerance I believe the story of Ruth is advocating, for without tolerance, the great King David—in whose lineage the promised Messiah would come—would not even have qualified as Jewish.

So, Ruth was written to oppose intolerance and exclusiveness among the faith community—to oppose

---

[9] Dictionary.com, "Tolerance," accessed February 21, 2026, https://www.dictionary.com/browse/tolerance.

bigotry. And that is what we are called to oppose today in the church and in our world.

William Sloane Coffin was the Yale University chaplain in the early seventies and later served as the senior pastor of Riverside Church in New York City. In response to questions of faith, Coffin said:

> *The one absolute is love. The integrity of love is much more important than the purity of dogma. I think dogma is a signpost, not a hitching post. It's always pointing beyond itself to God, and my problem with [many today] is they tend to put the purity of dogma ahead of the integrity of love and end up quite loveless in many instances.*

Then Coffin explains:

> *I think it's fair to say you can build community out of seekers of the truth, but you can't build community out of possessors of truth because they're also possessed of a certain hatred toward those who don't possess the truth, or who possess another truth than theirs.*[10]

I think we worship a God of such divine incomprehensibility that to say we speak for God takes more gall than we should probably allow ourselves. In my deepest thoughts and feelings, we can only say this is how I think it ought to be. But love is the plumb line that will measure these things. Now, if you believe that, you don't have to hang on to absolute truth with a white-knuckle grip. You're available for deeper meanings that may come your way.

Sometimes, thankfully, we do transcend our locks on the truth and our intolerance, and we not only tolerate but also go on to engage in dialogue, to genuine acceptance and even

---

[10] William Sloane Coffin, Jr., *The Heart Is a Little to the Left: Personal Excursions Beyond the Echo Chamber* (Louisville, KY: Westminster John Knox Press, 2002).

appreciation of one another's perspectives, backgrounds, and cultures. We become available for these deeper meanings in life. Not only did Boaz marry Ruth, but through her great-grandson, David, all of Judaism embraced and canonized her. So her message to us is to be tolerant so that acceptance, appreciation, and even love might eventually result and grow into a love without limits.

John Wesley characterized all of this so well in his sermon on the catholic spirit. Wesley says:

> *I do not mean, "Be of my opinion." You need not. Neither do I mean, "I will be of your opinion." I cannot. Keep you your opinion; I, mine, and that as steadily as ever. You need not even endeavor to come over to me or bring me over to you. I do not desire that. Let all opinions alone on one side and the other. But if thine heart is as my heart, if thou lovest God and all humankind, I ask no more: "Give me thine hand."*[11]

In other words, be tolerant! Love without limits!

Indeed, today, as the Body of Christ, we are called to be an inclusive—not an exclusive—fellowship and community. And today (as we do every day), we witness to that fact as surely as Ruth did.

Prayer:

God of wide mercy, teach us to love beyond our fears and our boundaries. Open our hearts to welcome the stranger, honor faithfulness wherever it is found, and live out a love that makes room for all. Shape us into a community that reflects your grace without limits. Amen.

---

[11] John Wesley, "Catholic Spirit," in *The Works of John Wesley*, Sermon 39.

Reflection Questions:

1. Where do you see yourself in the story of Ruth right now—as the outsider seeking belonging, the companion offering loyalty, or the community deciding who is welcomed? What does that reveal about your own faith journey?

2. What "boundaries" or assumptions might limit how you understand who belongs in God's community? How does Ruth's story challenge those limits?

3. What would it look like for you to practice love without limits this week? Who might God be inviting you to see, welcome, or stand alongside in a new way?

About the Writer:

Stella Roberts is a retired United Methodist elder who served forty-one years in active ministry, pastoring churches in Tennessee, West Virginia, and New Jersey. In addition to local church ministry, she served as a district superintendent and as director of Connectional Ministry.

CHAPTER EIGHT

Abigail

Wisdom in the Heat of Conflict

By Teresa Angle-Young

Scripture Lesson: 1 Samuel 25:2-42

> *There was a man in Maon whose property was in Carmel. The man was very rich; he had three thousand sheep and a thousand goats. He was shearing his sheep in Carmel. Now the man's name was Nabal, and his wife's name was Abigail. The woman was clever and beautiful, but the man was surly and mean; he was a Calebite. David heard in the wilderness that Nabal was shearing his sheep. So David sent ten young men, and David said to the young men, "Go up to Carmel, and go to Nabal, and greet him in my name. Thus you shall salute him, 'Peace be to you, and peace be to your house, and peace be to all that you have. I hear that you have shearers; now your shepherds have been with us, and we did them no harm, and they missed nothing all the time they were in Carmel. Ask your young men, and they will tell you. Therefore let my young men find favor in your sight, for we have come on a feast day. Please give whatever you have at hand to your servants and to your son David."*
>
> *When David's young men came, they said all this to Nabal in the name of David, and then they waited. But Nabal answered David's servants, "Who is David? Who is the son of Jesse? There are many servants today who are breaking away from their masters. Shall I take my bread and my water and the meat that I have butchered for my shearers and give it to men who come from I do not know where?" So David's young men turned away and came back and told him all this. David said to his men, "Every man strap on his sword!" And every one of them strapped on his sword; David also strapped on his sword, and about four hundred men went up after David, while two hundred remained with the baggage.*

But one of the young men told Abigail, Nabal's wife, "David sent messengers out of the wilderness to salute our master, and he shouted insults at them. Yet the men were very good to us, and we suffered no harm, and we never missed anything when we were in the fields as long as we were with them; they were a wall to us both by night and by day, all the while we were with them keeping the sheep. Now, therefore, know this and consider what you should do, for evil has been decided against our master and against all his house; he is so ill-natured that no one can speak to him."

Then Abigail hurried and took two hundred loaves, two skins of wine, five sheep ready dressed, five measures of parched grain, one hundred clusters of raisins, and two hundred cakes of figs. She loaded them on donkeys and said to her young men, "Go on ahead of me; I am coming after you." But she did not tell her husband Nabal. As she rode on the donkey and came down under cover of the mountain, David and his men came down toward her, and she met them. Now David had said, "Surely it was in vain that I protected all that this fellow has in the wilderness, so that nothing was missed of all that belonged to him, but he has returned me evil for good. God do so to David and more also if by morning I leave so much as one male of all who belong to him."

When Abigail saw David, she hurried and dismounted from the donkey and fell before David on her face, bowing to the ground. She fell at his feet and said, "Upon me alone, my lord, be the guilt; please let your servant speak in your ears and hear the words of your servant. My lord, do not take seriously this ill-natured fellow, Nabal, for as his name is, so is he; Nabal is his name, and folly is with him, but I, your servant, did not see the young men of my lord, whom you sent.

"Now then, my lord, as the Lord lives and as you yourself live, since the Lord has restrained you from bloodguilt and from taking vengeance with your own hand, now let your enemies and those who seek to do evil to my lord be like Nabal. And now let this present that your servant has brought to my lord be given to the young men who follow my lord. Please forgive the trespass of your servant, for the Lord will certainly make my lord a sure house, because my lord is fighting the battles of the Lord, and evil shall not be found in you so long as you live. If anyone should rise

up to pursue you and to seek your life, the life of my lord shall be bound in the bundle of the living under the care of the Lord your God, but the lives of your enemies he shall sling out as from the hollow of a sling. When the Lord has done to my lord according to all the good that he has spoken concerning you and has appointed you prince over Israel, my lord shall have no cause of grief or pangs of conscience for having shed blood without cause or for having saved himself. And when the Lord has dealt well with my lord, then remember your servant."

David said to Abigail, "Blessed be the Lord, the God of Israel, who sent you to meet me today! Blessed be your good sense, and blessed be you, who kept me today from bloodguilt and from avenging myself by my own hand! For as surely as the Lord the God of Israel lives, who has restrained me from hurting you, unless you had hurried and come to meet me, truly by morning there would not have been left to Nabal so much as one male." Then David received from her hand what she had brought him; he said to her, "Go up to your house in peace; see, I have heeded your voice, and I have granted your petition."

Abigail came to Nabal; he was holding a feast in his house like the feast of a king. Nabal's heart was merry within him, for he was very drunk, so she told him nothing at all until the morning light. In the morning, when the wine had gone out of Nabal, his wife told him these things, and his heart died within him; he became like a stone. About ten days later the Lord struck Nabal, and he died.

When David heard that Nabal was dead, he said, "Blessed be the Lord, who has judged the case of Nabal's insult to me and has kept back his servant from evil; the Lord has returned the evildoing of Nabal upon his own head." Then David sent word to Abigail to make her his wife. When David's servants came to Abigail at Carmel, they said to her, "David has sent us to you to take you to him as his wife." She rose and bowed down, with her face to the ground, and said, "Your servant is a slave to wash the feet of the servants of my lord." Abigail got up hurriedly and rode away on a donkey; her five maids attended her. She went after the messengers of David and became his wife.

1 Samuel 25:2-42 (NRSVue)

The story of Abigail enters the biblical narrative like a breath of cool air on a scorching desert day. While the surrounding chapters pulse with tension—Saul hunting David, David gathering followers, rivalries sparring in the wilderness—Abigail appears quietly, changing the tone and timbre of the atmosphere. And yet her presence changes everything.

Her husband, Nabal, is introduced as a harsh, ill-natured, and badly behaved man. The Hebrew word behind "ill-natured," הֶשָׁק qasheh, suggests someone stubborn, unyielding, and hard-hearted. His wealth is significant, but so is his propensity for foolish decisions and insolence, and Scripture wastes no time showing us the contrast between the couple. Abigail is described as "intelligent and beautiful"—a pairing rare in biblical introductions. But her beauty is not just physical. It radiates from her discernment, her capacity to read a volatile situation, and her courage to respond decisively with wisdom.

When David's men approach Nabal with a reasonable and respectful request for provisions, Nabal responds with contempt: "Who is David?" His insult is not only personal; it is political. David is an emerging leader, beloved by many, running from a king who fears him. Nabal's refusal is more than a sting. It's a provocation. And David, already weary from grief and injustice, snaps. He arms four hundred men and heads toward Nabal's household in a cloud of fury. The text does not soften David's state of mind; he intends to kill every male in Nabal's camp by morning.

Into this violent trajectory steps Abigail.

She learns what has happened and, without waiting for Nabal's direction or permission, gathers food, wine, and provisions. Her movements are urgent but not chaotic. She assembles bread, roasted grain, raisin cakes, and meat—an abundant feast, not a token gesture. She sends the servants ahead and follows after them. The text slows at this point, almost reverently, as if to let us hold our breath. This is storytelling at its finest, creating a dramatic pause and a sense of anticipation.

Abigail descends a hidden ravine and meets David and his armed men head-on.

The moment is astonishing. David is furious, armed, wronged, and marching with lethal intent. Abigail is unarmed, riding a donkey, carrying only provisions and courage.

Yet she does not tremble.

When she sees David, she dismounts and falls at his feet, not out of fear, but out of resolve. She chooses humility not as submission, but as a strategy. She speaks with clarity, dignity, and theological insight. Her speech is one of the longest of any woman in the historical books of Scripture.

She first takes responsibility—not because she is guilty, but because she understands what intelligent leaders have always known: that conflict often requires someone willing to hold what others will not or cannot carry. She then acknowledges Nabal's behavior, calling it foolish, to try to protect her household from bloodshed. She then affirms David's calling, reminding him of the promise God has placed upon his life. And finally, she invites him to consider his future self: When the Lord has fulfilled all his promises to you ... you will not have on your conscience the staggering burden of needless bloodshed.

Her wisdom cuts through David's rage. She gives him

something he desperately needs in this moment: perspective. She offers him a vision of himself grounded not in vengeance but in vocation. Abigail helps David see beyond his anger to his purpose.

And David listens.

He blesses her, blesses her discernment, and blesses her for keeping him from shedding blood. The turning point of the story is not David's anger or Nabal's foolishness; it is Abigail's intervention. Her courage redirects a violent future into a peaceful one.

A few days later, when Nabal dies unexpectedly, David remembers her. He sends for her—not as a trophy of conquest but recognizing her wisdom—as someone he wants near him. She becomes one of David's wives, and though the ancient context of marriage looks different from our own, the narrative treats Abigail with honor and dignity. She remains a symbol of discernment, poised leadership, and moral clarity.

Abigail's Emotional Intelligence

What makes Abigail even more compelling is the emotional intelligence (EQ) she displays under extreme pressure. Long before psychology gave us language like *self-regulation*, *empathy*, and *social awareness*, Abigail was living them.

She embodies self-awareness by recognizing the emotional temperature of the moment—David's fury, Nabal's arrogance, her household's vulnerability—and locating her own role within it. She does not panic or collapse. She understands how her presence and her posture will be perceived and uses that knowledge wisely.

Her self-regulation is remarkable. David's soldiers are armed. Dust swirls. Tension hangs in the air. Yet Abigail does not mirror the chaos. She speaks in measured phrases, grounded and calm. She chooses her tone with intention, demonstrating that steady presence is often the first step toward de-escalation.

Her empathy is apparent in the way she speaks to David. She does not shame him. She understands why he is angry. She sees his wounds, his frustrations, and his sense of betrayal. She speaks into the part of him that feels unseen and unjustly treated. She basically says, "I see you. I really see you, David."

Her social awareness helps her read the layers of power, gender, culture, and danger at play. She knows when and how to approach and which words will disarm rather than provoke. She navigates the complexity with incredible grace.

Her relationship wisdom truly shines in the way she nudges David toward his better self. She reminds him of God's calling, not his immediate grievance. She helps him imagine a future he can live with. In this way, she practices emotional intelligence not simply for survival, but for transformation.

Abigail's statement about Nabal—"as his name is, so is he"—carries more weight than a casual insult. In Hebrew, *Nabal* literally means "fool," not in the sense of lacking intelligence, but in the deeper biblical sense of someone who refuses wisdom, ignores God's ways, and acts with reckless disregard for others. Abigail is not slandering her husband; she is naming the reality of his character so David will not take Nabal's offense as a reflection of her household as a whole. By acknowledging Nabal's foolishness out loud, she releases David from the need to avenge his pride. Her words act like a pressure valve, letting the steam out of David's anger before it can do harm. In naming Nabal's folly, she protects both her people and David's future.

Then she adds, "I, your servant, did not see the young men of my lord." With this, Abigail gently communicates that the situation could have unfolded differently had she been involved sooner. She creates emotional distance from Nabal's behavior without distancing herself from responsibility. It is a subtle but masterful move in conflict de-escalation: she validates David's feelings, acknowledges the wrong that was done, and makes clear that his anger is understandable—yet she challenges the idea that violence is the necessary response. Her words show David a path that is both honest and merciful. In this moment, Abigail models the kind of emotional intelligence that sees clearly, speaks truthfully, and acts redemptively.

Modeling Abigail's Emotional Intelligence Today

Abigail's story invites us to cultivate the same kind of emotional intelligence in our own lives, not as a technique for manipulation, but as a spiritual discipline rooted in wisdom and peacemaking.

We model Abigail's EQ when we practice:

- **Staying grounded when others escalate:** She teaches us that we can choose our tone even when we cannot choose our circumstances.
- **Reading the room with compassion:** Abigail perceives the deeper story beneath David's anger.

We, too, can learn to look beyond the surface—to ask what pain, insecurity, or longing might be driving someone's behavior.

- **Using courage and calm together:** Abigail's bravery is not reckless; it is thoughtful. Emotional intelligence helps us approach conflict without hostility and honesty without unnecessary harm.
- **Speaking to someone's identity rather than their actions:** She reminds David who he is *becoming* and what God has planned for him. When we affirm someone's calling—rather than attacking their mistakes—we help them rise to their best self.
- **Acting before more resentment builds:** Abigail doesn't wait for perfect conditions. She moves quickly to create a pathway to peace. Emotional intelligence helps us intervene wisely rather than reactively.
- **Choosing humility without abandoning dignity:** Her posture is low, but her presence is strong. Emotional intelligence helps us balance courage with gentleness.

Ultimately, Abigail shows us that spiritual maturity and emotional maturity are deeply intertwined. She models a way of living in which wisdom is not withdrawn or passive but actively shapes the world toward mercy, clarity, and peace.

Abigail's story shows us that emotional intelligence is far more than a modern skill set. It becomes a spiritual witness. The way we interpret events, respond to others, and manage our own reactions reveals what we believe about God's character, human dignity, our own worth, and the sacredness of others. When we cultivate this kind of grounded wisdom, we step into the world as agents of reconciliation, carrying a peace that does not waver in the face of conflict.

In *Difficult Conversations: How to Discuss What Matters Most,*[12] authors Stone, Patton, and Heen describe how every hard exchange contains three overlapping conversations: the "what happened" conversation, the "feelings" conversation, and the "identity" conversation. Abigail instinctively moves through all three. She names the facts without defensiveness, honors the emotions in the room— especially David's wounded pride—and speaks to his deeper identity as a future king who will not want bloodshed on his conscience. By attending to each layer, she shifts the encounter away from escalation and toward what the authors call a "learning conversation," the kind that opens space for understanding, healing, and renewal rather than destruction and relational damage.

Abigail steps into Scripture only for a moment, yet she leaves behind a model of courage, clarity, and emotionally grounded wisdom that still speaks with surprising strength. She reminds us that the holiest work is often done in the tension between destruction and hope, where someone must choose humility over pride and discernment over impulse. Her intervention becomes a turning point not because she has power, but because she uses what she has—presence, insight, and compassion—to call forth the best in another person. When we follow her example, we learn that wisdom is not passive; it is active, brave, and creative. It interrupts harm, widens the path of peace, and reveals a God who honors those who choose reconciliation over retaliation.

---

[12] Douglas Stone, Bruce Patton, and Sheila Heen, *Difficult Conversations: How to Discuss What Matters Most,* 3rd ed. (New York: Penguin Books, 2023).

Prayer:

God of wisdom and peace, thank you for Abigail, whose calm presence, clear mind, and courageous heart turned anger away and opened the path to life. Teach us to cultivate the same emotional steadiness in our own lives. Give us the self-awareness to recognize what is happening within us, the empathy to understand what others carry, and the discernment to speak truth with grace. When conflict rises, make us people who stay grounded, who bless rather than provoke, and who help others remember who they are at their best. Shape our emotional lives so that they reflect your character: patient, compassionate, and merciful. Amen.

Reflection Questions:

1. Abigail remains steady even when David arrives in anger. Where in your life do you most struggle to stay grounded when others escalate? What helps you regulate your own emotions?

2. Emotional intelligence begins with self-awareness. How do you typically respond in moments of conflict? Fight, flight, freeze, or something else? What would Abigail's example invite you to notice?

3. Abigail shows deep empathy for David, even when he is in the wrong. How does empathy change the way you interpret others' behavior, especially when they are acting out of pain or fear?

4. Abigail speaks to David's identity, his calling, and his future, rather than attacking his anger. How might shifting your focus from someone's actions to their deeper potential reshape your relationships?

5. Abigail acts quickly but thoughtfully, choosing humility without losing her dignity. How might you practice that same blend of courage and gentleness in a current situation that needs wisdom?

6. In what ways does emotional intelligence serve as a spiritual practice for you? How might emotional intelligence deepen your discipleship and mirror the peacemaking character of God?

About the Writer:

Teresa Angle-Young is a United Methodist elder, writer, and speaker whose body of work focuses on spiritual formation, leadership, and the practice of attentive living. She is co-author, with Jessie Squires Colwell, of the devotional *Creation's Call,* which invites readers into deeper engagement with the natural world and the work of creation care.

CHAPTER NINE

What Are You Willing to Risk for a Moment Like This?

By Kay Kotan

Scripture Lesson: Esther 4:10-16

> *Then Esther spoke to Hathach and gave him a message for Mordecai: "All the king's servants and the people of the king's provinces know that, if any man or woman goes to the king inside the inner court without being called, there is but one law: to be put to death. Only if the king holds out the golden scepter to someone may that person live. I myself have not been called to come in to the king for thirty days." When they told Mordecai what Esther had said, Mordecai told them to reply to Esther, "Do not think that in the king's palace you will escape any more than all the other Jews. For if you keep silent at this time, relief and deliverance will rise for the Jews from another place, but you and your father's family will perish. Who knows? Perhaps you have come to royal dignity for just such a time as this." Then Esther said in reply to Mordecai, "Go, gather all the Jews to be found in Susa, and hold a fast on my behalf, and neither eat nor drink for three days, night or day. I and my maids will also fast as you do. After that I will go to the king, though it is against the law, and if I perish, I perish."*
>
> **Esther 4:10-16 (NRSVue)**

When was the last time you were asked to do something beyond your comfort zone? Step out of your natural tendencies, life's typical rhythms, and safe practices? When was the last time you took a real risk? Tried something new?

As we age, we tend to live life more safely. Throughout

our years, we have had experiences that have resulted in less-than-desirable outcomes. We suffer from our poor choices. We live life and learn. We gain wisdom. However, sometimes those less-than-desirable lived experiences create a tendency to play life safe—or at least safer. We create a safe bubble to live without (or with limited) risks or dangers. While there is some logic to this approach, what opportunities and experiences do we miss when we play life too safe, when life becomes too comfortable?

Let me be honest. I am sometimes guilty of playing it too safe. I talk myself out of trying something new or taking on a new experience because I don't want to endure the steep learning curve required. Or, I convince myself that the hassle of participation is just not worth any possible outcome. Or, the energy and time it will take is too much. Or, my fear of what awful thing *might* happen wins the day! I tend to rely on my life's motto of "fake it till you make it" less and less often as I age. I find myself more attracted to the least risky choices in life.

My husband is a risk-taker. He is a skydiver and parasailer. In his professional life, he repeatedly stretched every corporate policy and procedure "for the sake of the customer." He drove extremely fast in his younger years and had the insurance premiums to prove it when we first met. He would tell you that I'm a risk-taker of a different breed. I don't waste time by arriving at places early. The speed limit is a suggestion—the "real" limit is seven to nine miles over the posted speed limit. As my husband and I clearly demonstrate, each person has a different risk definition and tolerance.

A good friend of our family is an accountant. Before his recent retirement, every business day was the same for him—like a *Groundhog Day* experience. Every Monday, he did his laundry and ironing. He packed the same lunch for decades—ham and cheese with mustard on white bread and an apple. At the same time every Friday, he ate at the same fast-food restaurant and ordered the same combo menu item. He had the same cereal every morning and ate it while he worked the crossword puzzle in the local newspaper. This man thrived on routine, a routine that was low-risk, low-stress, and comfortable.

How about you? What is your risk tolerance? Have you jumped out of an airplane? Bungee jumped? Climbed Mount Everest? Are you a roller-coaster enthusiast? Are you a thrill seeker? Are you the first to try a new restaurant? Are you an early adopter of breaking technology? What kind of risk-taker are you? Has it changed throughout the years?

In the story of Esther, risk-taking was certainly in play. The setting was about 480 BC in the Persian Empire. As you might recall, King Xerxes had bought into Haman's (who served in the king's court) story that there was this "odd set of people in the kingdom who didn't fit in." Haman had agreed to finance the operation if the king issued orders to have them destroyed. Little did the king know that his wife, Queen Esther, and her family were part of that "odd set of people" Haman described, which the king ordered destroyed.

Mordecai, Esther's uncle, who had raised her as his daughter, learned of the proclamation. He sent word to Esther that she must go to the king and intercede for her people.

> *Don't think for one minute that, unlike all the other Jews, you'll come out of this alive simply because you are in the palace.*

In fact, if you don't speak up at this very important time,
relief and rescue will appear for the Jews from another place,
but you and your family will die.
But who knows?
Maybe it was for a moment like this that you came to be part of the royal family.

Esther 4:10-14 (CEB)

Esther was petrified. Not only did the king not know her background, but she could be killed for approaching the king without invitation. Everyone knew that anyone who approached the king without first being invited would be put to death. The only exception is if the king extends his golden scepter in one's presence. It had been thirty days since Esther had been invited to come before the king.

Esther sent back this response to Mordecai's message:

Go, gather all the Jews who are in Susa and tell them to give up eating to help me be brave.

They aren't to eat or drink anything for three whole days, and I myself will do the same, along with my female servants.

Then, even though it's against the law, I will go to the king; and if I am to die, then die I will.

Esther 4:16 (CEB)

Esther risked being killed to go before the king. Yet, she proceeded with great bravery. She was very smart and strategic over a couple of dinners with both King Xerxes and Haman. Through her wise and intentional interactions during those dinners, Haman framed himself. In the end, Haman was actually hanged on the very gallows Haman had built for Mordecai's demise, and Mordecai and Esther's people were saved. Mordecai became part of the king's court, and Queen Esther inherited Haman's estate—all because Esther was willing to risk her very life!

Most risks we ponder come nowhere close to risking our lives—maybe our comfort, but not our lives. We find ourselves living in a hurting, broken, and divided world. Given today's hurting world, what are you willing to risk as a follower of Jesus? What were you placed to do for a moment like this?

Here are a few examples where followers of Jesus could step up and out of the church for greater impact:

- We find ourselves in a mental health crisis. Roughly one in three people currently suffer from mental illness, such as depression and anxiety. US Surgeon General Vivek Murthy argues that the country is experiencing an "epidemic of loneliness."[13]
    - Who in your life is experiencing mental illness? Who do you encounter who suffers from loneliness? How are you risking being a friend to them?
- Research suggests that many mothers report feeling underserved and unsupported by their churches, which can contribute to disengagement from church life.
    - What mom in your life could use some support? What mom do you know that would benefit from having a sense of community that you could offer or launch?

---

[13] U.S. Department of Health and Human Services, *Our Epidemic of Loneliness and Isolation: The U.S. Surgeon General's Advisory on the Healing Effects of Social Connection and Community* (Washington, DC, 2023).

- More than three-quarters of Americans are spiritually open.[14] However, how they access resources and community for their spiritual journey is changing in our TED Talk and TikTok world. Those who are spiritually open seek to explore their spirituality, ask questions without being judged, and form their own beliefs.
    - How might you engage with the spiritually open people in your life to journey with them as they discover their core being—beliefs, belonging, purpose, and impact?
- Research from the Pew Research Center shows that about one-third of U.S. adults no longer identify with the religion of their childhood, a shift many describe as faith deconstruction.[15]
    - Who are you coming alongside to support, mentor, and guide as they reconstruct their faith?

Risk is a matter of perspective. So much of the world's suffering stems from a single underlying issue: the lack of loving relationships. How much of a risk is it to invest in the life of another one of God's children? As a follower of Jesus, what are you willing to risk for such a time as this? As part of a congregation, what is the church willing to risk to truly love our neighbor as ourselves?

Do you remember this nostalgic nursery rhyme and the hand motions that went with it from your Sunday school days?

---

[14] Barna Group, "What Does It Mean to Be Spiritually Open?" *Barna*, June 21, 2023, https://www.barna.com/research/spiritual-openness/.

[15] Pew Research Center, *Why Americans Leave, Stay in Their Childhood Religion*, December 15, 2025, https://www.pewresearch.org/religion/2025/12/15/why-do-some-americans-leave-their-religion-while-others-stay.

Here's the church.
Here's the steeple.
Open the door, and
See all the people!

What did this simple rhyme teach you about the church? This rhyme taught me to believe that the church is the building. It also taught that to see "all" the people, one had to first open the church doors. This rhyme implied that to be seen, one would have to be assembled inside a church building. In this nursery rhyme's model of the church, there is no personal or congregational risk. It is a "come to us" model. And honestly, how is that really working out for the church? I'm not sure I believe the essence of this rhyme anymore, and I've had to deconstruct the lessons it taught me as a child. Some of us risk life and limb for thrill-seeking or our favorite hobbies. Esther was willing to risk her life to save her people! Jesus gave his life to save you and me. In a world full of people who are lonely, depressed, anxious, spiritually curious, and seeking support and a sense of community, the risk it might take to share Jesus with others is really quite minimal in comparison.

Would you be willing to risk some of your time and energy? Some of your life experiences? Sharing your life stories with others who might benefit?

Seriously, what are you willing to risk for such a time as this so that someone might come to know and love Jesus? And who knows, that person may one day be the very one who risks introducing your grandchild to Jesus! Think about that investment. Now, what are you willing to risk (invest) for a moment like this?

The Prayer of Esther

O my Lord, you alone are our King.
Come to my assistance,
for I am alone and have no one to help me but you.
My life is in great danger.
From my earliest days I was taught by my family that you,
O Lord, chose Israel out of all the nations
and our fathers from among all their forebearers,
as an everlasting heritage, and that you have fulfilled all the promises you made to them.
But now we have sinned against you,
and you have handed us over to our enemies
because we paid honor to their gods. You are just, O Lord.
However, now our enemies are not satisfied with our bitter slavery.
They have vowed to their idols to annul the decree you have proclaimedand destroy your heritage,
to silence the mouths of those who praise you
and to destroy your altar and the glory of your house,
and instead, to open the mouths of the nations
to praise their worthless idols and to offer an earthly king everlasting praise.

O Lord, do not consign your scepter to gods who do not exist.
Do not let our enemies exult in our downfall,
but turn their designs against them and make an example of the chief of our persecutors.
Remember us, O Lord. Reveal yourself in this time of our tribulation, and give me courage, O King of gods and Master of every dominion.
Give me the power of persuasive speech when I face the lion and enable me to turn his heart to hatred of the one who is our enemy so that he and all those who share his feelings may perish.
Save us by your arm and come to my aid, for I am alone and have no one on whom to rely but you, O Lord.

You know all things.

You are fully aware that I hate the honors offered by the

wicked and abhor the bed of the uncircumcised or of any alien.

You know the straits I am in.

I loathe the symbol of my proud position that I wear on my head on days when I appear in public. I detest it as if it were an unclean rag, and I do not wear it on days when I am in private.

I, your servant, have never eaten at Haman's table, nor have I attended any banquet of the king or drunk the wine of libations.

From the day I changed my state until now, I have experienced no joy except in you,

O Lord, God of Abraham.

O God all-powerful, give heed to the pleas of those in despair.

Deliver us from the power of the wicked and rescue me from my fear.

Esther 4:14-30 (NCB)

Prayer:

Lord God, for such a time as this, loosen our grip on comfort and steady our trembling hearts, that we might risk love, compassion, and courageous witness for the sake of those who are lonely, hurting, and spiritually searching. Give us Esther's bravery and Christ's self-giving spirit, so that through our willingness to step beyond safety, others may discover Your saving grace.

Reflection Questions:

1. What risk might you be willing to take so that one of God's children might come to know Jesus? How big a risk would this be for you? Please explain.

2. How could your life experiences be invested in others for kingdom purposes and impact? How big a risk would this be for you? Please explain.

3. What mark will Christ leave on the lives of those who don't know him today through you in such a time as this? What is Christ calling you to do for such a moment like this?

About the Writer:

Kay Kotan is the founder of You Unlimited. She is an accredited coach and a 15+ year church consultant. Kay spends her time investing in pastors, laity leaders, congregations, and judicatory leaders by equipping, coaching, and creating resources to help them discover and live into their fullest missional potential for effectiveness and fruitfulness in reaching people for Jesus Christ.

CHAPTER TEN

A Simple Touch

By Bishop Sharma D. Lewis Logan

Scripture Lesson: Mark 5:25-34

> *And a woman was there who had been subject to bleeding for twelve years. She had suffered a great deal under the care of many doctors and had spent all she had, yet instead of getting better, she grew worse. When she heard about Jesus, she came up behind him in the crowd and touched his cloak, because she thought, "If I just touch his clothes, I will be healed." Immediately, her bleeding stopped, and she felt in her body that she was freed from her suffering.*
>
> *At once, Jesus realized that power had gone out from him. He turned around in the crowd and asked, "Who touched my clothes?"*
>
> *"You see the people crowding against you," his disciples answered, "and yet you can ask, 'Who touched me?'"*
>
> *But Jesus kept looking around to see who had done it. Then the woman, knowing what had happened to her, came and fell at his feet and, trembling with fear, told him the whole truth. He said to her, "Daughter, your faith has healed you. Go in peace and be freed from your suffering."*
>
> **Mark 5:25-34 (NIV)**

Research has demonstrated that a *simple touch* can promote healing within the body in as little as minutes. Such a touch can provide encouragement, calm a fretful or teething baby, and offer comfort. In biblical times, regardless of age, social status, or background—whether young or old, rich or poor, Jew or Gentile—Jesus was unafraid to touch the untouchables.

This narrative is integrated into Jairus's daughter's story using intercalation, a literary technique that inserts one story within another, enhancing the depth and complexity of the overall account. Jesus demonstrates his authority over an incurable illness and even death itself. Scholars have classified both events as miracle stories. A miracle story typically has five characteristics: a problem or crisis that worsens, development of the problem or crisis, contact between key individuals, healing, and public confirmation of the miracle.

The Gospel of Mark indicates that Jesus crossed the Sea of Galilee again, probably landing in Capernaum. Jairus, a local ruler of the synagogue, summons Jesus, falls at his feet, and pleads for his help to heal his dying daughter. Jesus, without hesitation, goes, and a large multitude follows. What makes this story unique is its interruption by a nameless woman who has suffered from a hemorrhage for twelve years.

I have always wondered why the gospel writers never gave this woman a name. Could this woman's story be any woman's story? Could it be that when we are faced with a crisis, a name, socioeconomic status, or age is irrelevant?

This woman's story has served as a personal model of faith during my own struggles. I've come to realize that a simple touch of Jesus' faith can restore one to wholeness.

Mark recounts that the hemorrhaging woman endured many treatments from many physicians, yet her condition worsened. This incurable condition may have been a menstrual or uterine disorder, which would have made her ritually unclean and socially ostracized.

According to Leviticus 15:19-27, anyone or anything she touched would be ceremonially defiled until the evening, requiring the person she touched to wash their clothes and bathe in water. In addition, according to ancient Jewish writings, there were as many as eleven different cures for bleeding; however, in this case, the woman was incurable. Can you imagine being this woman? She must have been waging a personal war inside her. She was weak from continuous blood loss, financially depleted after exhausting all of her resources, and socially ostracized due to the customs of the day. I imagine she would lie in bed questioning—how long, Lord, will I suffer? I'm tired of feeling both hopeful and hopeless. I'm tired of wondering, is this the day the bleeding will stop?

Her story underscores that even in despair, faith can inspire action. The nameless woman's faith led her to seek the Lord for herself. There was likely a sense of excitement in the air as word spread that Jesus was nearby. Her determination to seek Jesus, despite her condition, exemplifies a proactive approach to her healing. She refused to give in to despair or let others dissuade her from seeking Jesus. Mark states that "she heard" about Jesus—about his healing power demonstrated through various miracles. Perhaps she heard how he had healed Peter's mother-in-law, the bent-over woman of eighteen years, the paralyzed man, the lame, and the mute.

- What have you heard about Jesus?
- He will change your rejection to redemption.
- He will change your tears to testimonies.
- He will change your valley experiences to victories.

While hearing about Jesus is crucial, our responsibility extends to sharing his story with others. Revelation 3:20 reminds us, "Here I am, I stand at the door and knock. If anyone hears my voice and opens the door, I will come in and eat with that person, and they with me" (NIV). On this day, the hemorrhaging woman's desperation drove her to ignore ritualistic restrictions, for she knew her bleeding would make Jesus ceremonially unclean.

Every day, we must ponder the question: Do we merely know *about* Jesus, or do we *know* Jesus for ourselves?

Mark 5:28 states, "If only I just touch his clothes, I will be healed" (NIV). She demonstrated her faith by pressing through difficulties to reach Jesus. I believe the woman discovered strength in her life that she did not know existed—strength to overcome the obstacles of pain, insecurity, loneliness, depression, and low self-esteem.

Do we press our way to touch the Master? I envision Jesus standing amidst the crowd with others blocking her view. Yet, with all her strength, she pushed past her fears and pain because she had suffered for twelve years and couldn't bear to let another twelve years pass by without change. The apostle Paul writes in Philippians 3:14, "I press toward the mark for the prize of the high calling of God in Christ Jesus" (KJV), which resonates here. The woman's act of pressing forward was rooted in humility and surrender—she believed that even touching the tassel of Jesus' garment could bring her healing.

Her simple act of faith—touching Jesus—resulted in immediate healing. When she touched him, power flowed out of Jesus, prompting him to ask his disciples, "Who touched me?" The disciples, overwhelmed by the crowd, might have thought this was a trivial question. Yet the woman, trembling, fell at Jesus' feet and acknowledged her act of faith. Instead of being defiled, her contact with Jesus proved more powerful than her incurable disease.

Mark's account confirms that she was healed immediately. Jesus responded with compassion, calling her "daughter," a term of endearment and a recognition of her place in the Kingdom. Commentaries reveal that this is the only place in Scripture where Jesus refers to someone as a daughter. He affirms that her faith—not his clothes—made her well. Her act was rooted in belief—claiming faith in action. Faith that remains dormant is ineffective, but genuine faith compels action. Faith calls us to release our reliance on ourselves and to place our trust wholly in God. Countless men and women brushed against Jesus, but only one woman's touch resulted in healing. As the gospel hymn reminds us, "He touched me and made me whole."[16]

Prayer:

Lord, help us to see that a simple touch of faith can lead to my wholeness. Amen.

---

[16] Bill Gaither, *He Touched Me*, 1963, gospel hymn.

Reflection Questions:

1. What themes particularly spoke to you in this narrative?

2. How do you think this woman lived after her miraculous healing?

3. What can we learn about keeping faith from remaining dormant? What action might you be compelled to take?

About the Writer:

Bishop Sharma D. Lewis Logan became the first African American woman to be elected bishop in the Southeastern Jurisdiction of The United Methodist Church in 2016. She is author and co-author of several books, including:

Ashes to Alleluia
Struggle to the Cross
Advent in Four Words
Journey to Transformation

CHAPTER ELEVEN

You Are Created with Power and Purpose

The Story of Mary, the Mother of Jesus

By Bishop LaTrelle Miller Easterling

Scripture Lesson: Luke 1:46-56

And Mary said, "My soul magnifies the Lord,
and my spirit rejoices in God my Savior,
for he has looked with favor on the lowly state of his servant.
Surely from now on all generations will call me blessed,
for the Mighty One has done great things for me,
and holy is his name;
indeed, his mercy is for those who fear him
from generation to generation.
He has shown strength with his arm;
he has scattered the proud in the imagination of their hearts.
He has brought down the powerful from their thrones
and lifted up the lowly;
he has filled the hungry with good things
and sent the rich away empty.
He has come to the aid of his child Israel,
in remembrance of his mercy,
according to the promise he made to our ancestors,
to Abraham and to his descendants forever."

Luke 1:46-56 (NRSVue)

Does my life have meaning? What is my purpose? Will my having lived make any difference at all? These are the perennial questions of life that have been asked across millennia by many, but especially by women. In too many places and spaces, women are still viewed as irrelevant or second-class citizens. In too many pulpits, women are still preached as simply the helpmeet of a man. In too many workplaces, women are undervalued and underpaid. In too many corners of the world, we are dismissed, demeaned, and denied. But this is not God's design nor desire. From Genesis to Revelation, we find women prominently included in God's divine plans. Moreover, as a woman of faith, I believe that everyone is created in the *Imago Dei,* the very image and likeness of God. We are not here by happenstance or accident; rather, when God knit us together in our mothers' wombs, it was done with intentionality. We were created with divine destiny and providential purpose. And God's purposes always bring liberation, elevation, love, and light. We are participants in breaking chains and shining light when we embody the power and purpose of our call. And so the question then becomes: when our purpose is revealed, will we have the courage to respond to God's call, or will we cower beneath the weight of culture? The story of Mary, the mother of Jesus, should inspire us to respond to God's call with a resounding **"Yes!"**

Scripture teaches us that Mary was a young woman of modest economic means. She was engaged to Joseph, but they had not yet wed. As was the custom in their day, a young woman was expected to be a virgin until her wedding night. Therefore, when the angel appeared to Mary and explained that she would conceive before her nuptials, she was understandably taken aback and questioned how this could be possible. Gabriel responded that she need not fear because she had found favor with God. The God of creation had chosen her to bring forth the one prophesied to liberate and elevate the lowly and fill those who hunger. As Mary heard these words and observed the glory hovering around her, she understood that she had been selected by God to be used for God's purpose. She understood the hand of providence that was upon her life. She understood that her womb would birth life and liberation. Mary understood her purpose. She then offered a hymn of praise to acknowledge God's call. Her Magnificat, her melodious *yes*, echoes through history as a lyrical lesson and a powerful testimony of what is possible when we walk in our purpose.

While some have chosen to interpret Mary's story as being representative of disempowerment, acquiescence, or even physical abuse, I see a different revelation. As I read her story, Mary stands as an example of empowerment and radical discipleship. It should be noted that although Mary existed at a time when women had no voice, no validation, no power, and a limited perceived purpose, she did not consult anyone before accepting God's call. Although she was engaged to Joseph, she did not seek his permission. Although she was still a young woman, she did not request her father's approval. Although she could anticipate becoming the subject of vicious gossip, she did not ask for her neighbors' understanding. Even though Mary stood to lose everything, including her very life, she said *yes* to God's inconceivable call.

I don't think we fully recognize Mary's fortitude. She understood herself as being beloved by God even before her annunciation. And let us not ignore that Mary exercised her voice and agency to ask Gabriel a question. She did not simply capitulate to the overwhelming presence of this angelic figure; rather, she asked how this prophecy would be made manifest in light of her reality. Society may have seen her as a poor Woman of Color, but she understood herself to be a servant of the Most High God. That required strength, self-differentiation, and courage.

As women, too many in the world still try to convince us that we need permission to actualize our purpose, that our call must be validated, and our voices must be moderated. But Mary stands as a witness that our prophetic purpose is not bestowed by humanity; rather, it is the Spirit's breath already alive within us—breathed into Eve's lungs at creation and mediated to us through our grandmothers, mothers, and other mothers who have created, curated, crafted, and cultivated spaces of inclusion, justice, and liberation throughout history. We are the daughters of Helenor Davisson, Anna Howard Shaw, and Jareena Lee, who preached with power long before any conference conferred credentials. We walk in the missionary lineage of Clementina Butler and Lois Parker, who made a plea to eight women in Boston to ensure their sisters in India had access to health care. We are the fire of Fannie Lou Hamer, who was sick and tired of being sick and tired, and still sang freedom's song through a bruised jaw and a broken system. We are the prayers of Sojourner Truth, who asked, "Ain't I a woman?" and dared America to answer with integrity. We are the fierce love of countless women who may not have had titles, but had tenacity, who may not have had pulpits, but preached with their very lives. We must bear witness to the fact that God continues to call women as vessels to preach, teach, lead, heal, write, mediate, and be sent as missionaries. We must bear witness to the fact that when women of faith live into the power and purpose of their call, the earth shifts, and lives are changed.

Dr. Katalin Karikó, a biochemist and immigrant from

Hungary, received the Nobel Peace Prize in Physiology or Medicine in 2023 for her groundbreaking work that helped develop the COVID-19 vaccine. But Karikó's journey was fraught with skepticism, difficulty, and hardship. While many in her scientific community focused on DNA, she believed great strides could be made through work with RNA. As a child, she had a hunger for science, placing third in a science competition. Her quest to have the freedom to research, create, and contribute led her family to immigrate to the United States. Yet even in this country, her work was discouraged. The powers that be demanded that she shift her focus, but Karikó believed her focus was correct and would lead to breakthroughs. She was demoted, dismissed, and denied tenure for refusing to be dissuaded. Through providence, she met another scientist who understood her quest and valued her research. Together, they laid the groundwork for the vaccines that saved millions of lives. Today, Karikó holds sixteen patents, is highly respected as a visionary in science, and has been recognized by the very institutions that once discouraged her efforts. Dr. Katalin Karikó walked in her power and purpose, and the world benefited from her courage.

The Magnificat is the song of Mary after her holy surrender to the call of God. But let us make no mistake, Mary's song is not a lullaby. It is a revolution set to a melody. When this young, poor, unmarried girl from the wrong side of the tracks opened her mouth, empires trembled. They trembled because she was not singing the songs prescribed to women who remain in their place; she was prophesying about systems overturned and power structures reversed. She was singing about a countercultural revolution about to be born into the world. She was singing about a force that would not cower in timidity to the oppressive forces of empire. Hear the words of her freedom song, "He has brought down the powerful from their thrones, and lifted up the lowly; He has filled the hungry with good things and sent the rich away empty" (Luke 1:52-53, NRSVue). This is not sentimental fantasy; this is subversive faith. Mary's Magnificat is the anthem of women who refuse to let patriarchy, racism, oppression, culture, or empire have the last word. This is Mary walking in her power and her purpose.

Scholars remind us that when Mary sings, she preaches and interprets her own experience as divine revelation. In her body, God's Word becomes flesh; in her song, God's justice takes shape. Mary declares that God's call is never neutral. God has taken a side, and that side is with the poor, the displaced, the silenced, the abused, and the forgotten. So when she spoke, the earth shifted, not because she had institutional power, but because she had divine purpose. Too often, beloved, we have been told to wait for permission, to wait for confirmation, to wait for validation, to wait for affirmation, to wait until someone who lives in the façade of privilege and patriarchy tells us we can move. But I write to remind you that the Spirit has already signed your credentials. The Potter's hand has already given permission by the very fact that you have been shaped, anointed, and filled with God's power.

This reading of Mary's story is not just an alternative exegetical exercise; it is a holy unearthing. It is a sanctified confirmation of what God has already placed within you. We are digging through the sediment of social expectations, cultural stereotypes, and ecclesial hesitation to reclaim an ancient truth: women have, are, and will always be called as prophets of the Most High God, disciples of divine destiny, vessels of ancient wisdom, and co-creators with God. And just as the world needed the Savior who would be born of Mary, the world is groaning for what God has purposed for your life. There is still so much yet to be done. In poverty, mothers in Jackson, Mississippi, still cannot trust the water that runs through their taps. Families in Baltimore live in food deserts, miles from fresh fruit and vegetables. Villages in Sudan and Haiti starve while nations argue over aid. Mothers in Palestine and Kyiv are watching their babies draw their last breath because hospitals are being bombed, and supplies are rotting at roadblocks. God used Mary to bring liberation into the world because God said, **"Enough!"**

Those who believe that freedom cannot wait must answer the call and shout, "**Enough!**" In politics, where truth is being bartered for votes, where the marginalized are scapegoated as the powerful fill their coffers, where democracy teeters under the weight of authoritarianism and Christian Nationalism, those who believe that freedom cannot wait must answer their call and shout, "**Enough!**" In prisons where mass incarceration remains the new plantation, where living conditions are deplorable, rehabilitation has been abandoned in favor of retribution, and more children are being tried as adults, those who believe that freedom cannot wait must answer their call and shout, "**Enough!**" In healthcare, where disparities in maternal health persist, where mental illness is yet criminalized, and where the impoverished must choose between insulin and rent, those who believe that freedom cannot wait must answer their call and shout, "**Enough!**" In education, where children in underfunded schools learn under leaking ceilings, where books are being banned and the hallways turned into militarized zones, and where teachers are being penalized for teaching the truth of world history, those who believe that freedom cannot wait must rise and shout, "**Enough!**" In creation itself, where the land is weary from extraction and the seas are swollen with waste, refuse, and debris, the cry of those who believe that freedom, justice, righteousness, and mercy cannot wait must rise and shout, "**Enough!**"

You see, when those called by God to be vessels of righteousness won't live their calling, injustice thrives. When we silence our voices, oppression gets comfortable. But when women of faith remember their divine inheritance, systems tremble. Women have always been at the forefront. Women of power and purpose have lifted the weary, clothed the naked, educated children, and stood on the frontlines of justice. Women of power and purpose have embodied the Magnificat in action. But in this moment of global unrest, where democracy teeters, where rights are being rolled back, where wars rage, where Black, Brown, and Queer bodies are still endangered, where truth is being traded for convenience, the world needs prophetic voices more than ever.

Bishop Leontyne Kelly, the first African American woman elected to the episcopacy in The United Methodist Church, shifted the atmosphere. She answered her call when the church was unsure if it was ready to receive her. She answered when her very election was an act of holy defiance. And because she answered, the ground beneath our denomination moved. Bishop Kelly's very presence awakened generations of women who could now see themselves as leaders, general secretaries, superintendents, and bishops. She shattered a glass ceiling that enabled more women, but especially Women of Color, to see themselves in a new light. This is what occurs when you walk in your power and your purpose.

Although I was raised in a home where my mother was very involved in the church, often leading committees and even serving on a general agency, it wasn't until I saw ordained women in the pulpit that I began to understand the fullness of God's calling upon my life. It is important and empowering to see others from our demographic walking in their call. As women, we also often fear what we risk when we live lives of power and purpose. Will we be rejected or misunderstood? Will we be accused of stepping outside of our place? But we must also understand that the God who calls us also makes a way for us. As Gabriel was revealing God's plan to Mary, an angel was also preparing Joseph for what was to come. As a door closed in my life with a husband who could not accept my call, God was preparing my current life and ministry partner for what lay ahead. God's call will never send us where God's love and divine protection will not hold us. Even if you cannot see the end of the road, know that God has prepared the way. Do not be afraid to walk in your power and your purpose, for the God of Mary, Elizabeth, Anna, Jareena, and countless others is with you.

May this be our holy reawakening, not to an unfamiliar beckoning, but to the ancient call that has always lived in our bones. May this be our holy reawakening, not to an unfamiliar beckoning, but to the ancient call that has always lived in our bones. Because, believed, we are not called to echo the rhetoric of empire. Because, beloved, we are not called to echo the rhetoric of empire. We are called to embody the Kingdom. Not to replicate the systems that oppress, but to reveal the God who liberates. And when we do, when we speak truth to power, when we love fiercely and lead courageously, when we nurture and confront, build and tear down, the earth will shift again.

So, sisters, rise up like Mary and sing your Magnificat in a world desperate for melody. If God could bring a Savior and salvation through the womb of a woman, what hope and help does God want to birth through you? What transformational blessing has God ordained for your life? Who will be inspired through your leadership? For when you walk in your power and purpose, whenever women walk in their power and purpose, the earth shifts, and heaven rejoices. Amen and amen!

Prayer:

Holy and Liberating God,

You formed us in your divine image and likeness, called us before we could speak, and filled us with purpose and power.

Silence the voices within us that say we are not enough, not worthy, not chosen.

Remind us that we are not prisoners of empire's limitations and that your call does not require perfection, but only our willingness to be your vessels.

Turn our lives into living Magnificats, songs that lift the lowly, disrupt false peace,

and testify to your justice, mercy, and love.

Use our voices to share your liberating word,

our hands to bring your help and healing,

our hearts to spread your unconditional love,

and our lives to proclaim that You are still at work in the world.

Do through us what only You can do.

In the name of Christ, our Prince of Peace, we pray.

Amen.

Reflection Questions:

1. When you sit quietly before God, what truth about your worth or calling do you find hardest to believe? Why do you doubt yourself?

2. What is God asking of you right now that feels costly or disruptive? What fears rise in you when you imagine saying yes?

3. How might God be calling you to disturb the false peace in your community for the sake of justice, truth, or healing?

About the Writer:

Bishop LaTrelle Miller Easterling is the episcopal leader of the Baltimore-Washington and Peninsula-Delaware Area. Easterling's assignment to the Baltimore-Washington Conference in 2016 was groundbreaking, as she is the first woman to lead that historic conference. Easterling currently serves as chair of the Council of Bishops' Anti-Racism Leadership Team, on the Immigration Task Force, and as a board member of the General Board of Church and Society. She was recognized as a Distinguished Alumna from Boston University School of Theology for her justice and advocacy ministry, and she received the Rainbow PUSH Trombone Award for faith in action. Easterling is a much sought-after speaker, preacher, poet, and writer. She is married to the Rev. Marion Easterling, Jr., and they are the proud parents of two sons.

CHAPTER TWELVE

A Story to Share

By Michelle J. Morris

Scripture Lesson: John 4:7-42

A Samaritan woman came to draw water, and Jesus said to her, "Give me a drink." (His disciples had gone to the city to buy food.) The Samaritan woman said to him, "How is it that you, a Jew, ask a drink of me, a woman of Samaria?" (Jews do not share things in common with Samaritans.) Jesus answered her, "If you knew the gift of God and who it is that is saying to you, 'Give me a drink,' you would have asked him, and he would have given you living water." The woman said to him, "Sir, you have no bucket, and the well is deep. Where do you get that living water? Are you greater than our ancestor Jacob, who gave us the well and with his sons and his flocks drank from it?" Jesus said to her, "Everyone who drinks of this water will be thirsty again, but those who drink of the water that I will give them will never be thirsty. The water that I will give will become in them a spring of water gushing up to eternal life." The woman said to him, "Sir, give me this water, so that I may never be thirsty or have to keep coming here to draw water."

Jesus said to her, "Go, call your husband, and come back." The woman answered him, "I have no husband." Jesus said to her, "You are right in saying, 'I have no husband,' for you have had five husbands, and the one you have now is not your husband. What you have said is true!" The woman said to him, "Sir, I see that you are a prophet. Our ancestors worshiped on this mountain, but you say that the place where people must worship is in Jerusalem." Jesus said to her, "Woman, believe me, the hour is coming when you will worship the Father neither on this mountain nor in Jerusalem. You worship what you do not know; we worship what we know, for salvation is from the Jews. But the hour is coming and is now here when the true worshipers will worship the Father in spirit and truth, for the Father seeks such as these to worship him. God is spirit, and those who worship him must worship in spirit and truth." The woman said to him, "I know that the Messiah is coming" (who is called Christ). "When he comes, he will proclaim all things to us." Jesus said to her, "I am he, the one who is speaking to you."

Just then his disciples came. They were astonished that he was speaking with a woman, but no one said, "What do you want?" or, "Why are you speaking with her?" Then the woman left her water jar and went back to the city. She said to the people, "Come and see a man who told me everything I have ever done! He cannot be the Messiah, can he?" They left the city and were on their way to him.

Meanwhile the disciples were urging him, "Rabbi, eat something." But he said to them, "I have food to eat that you do not know about." So the disciples said to one another, "Surely no one has brought him something to eat?" Jesus said to them, "My food is to do the will of him who sent me and to complete his work. Do you not say, 'Four months more, then comes the harvest'? But I tell you, look around you, and see how the fields are ripe for harvesting. The reaper is already receiving wages and is gathering fruit for eternal life, so that sower and reaper may rejoice together. For here the saying holds true, 'One sows and another reaps.' I sent you to reap that for which you did not labor. Others have labored, and you have entered into their labor."

Many Samaritans from that city believed in him because of the woman's testimony, "He told me everything I have ever done." So when the Samaritans came to him, they asked him to stay with them, and he stayed there two days. And many more believed because of his word. They said to the woman, "It is no longer because of what you said that we believe, for we have heard for ourselves, and we know that this is truly the Savior of the world."

(John 4:7-42, NRSVue)

Have you ever had a rumor spread about you? Rumors take on a life of their own. Once they are out there, it can be very difficult to regain control of the narrative. In this day and age, rumors can wrap the world in a matter of seconds, spread across what is very appropriately named the World Wide Web, and you become caught like an insect to be devoured by people making all kinds of assumptions and spreading stories, whether they are actually based on facts or not.

Rumors become difficult to counter, even when you have written evidence to the contrary. I blame our brains. Our brains are only built to process a small fragment of the information we encounter at any given time. So sometimes our brains take a small detail and then mold it into what makes the most sense to us, or, quite honestly, what makes the best story. Then, once the brain has heard that story, it becomes almost impossible to dislodge with facts. What we really want to replace it with is a better story.

Want a couple of small examples of how this works? Here's one. I am routinely called "Melissa" by others. I think people hear me start to say my name, hear the "M" sound, and then promptly remember some woman's name that begins with M, which, for some reason, about half the time is Melissa. Now, here is a weird detail. I have had people call me Melissa in an online chat, where the only thing they have to refer to me is my printed name in the chat. It could not be clearer: "Michelle"!

Another example? What fruit did Adam and Eve eat in the Garden? You probably said an apple, but why? We are never told in the biblical text that the fruit is an apple. But your brain has seen it in paintings and on advertisements, and so an apple it is! I won't try to further mess with your brain and tell you that Eve actually didn't have her name yet when she ate the fruit, so even saying Adam and Eve ate the fruit is not exactly accurate.

I bring all of this up because we are reading the story of the Woman at the Well, and like many women of the Bible, all kinds of stories are told about her that are just not true—or at least cannot be confirmed. She has a particularly hard time because the text hints at rumors about her, and then we spread even more rumors about her outside the text! She is doubly a victim of gossip! Thankfully, Jesus came along to set her free from all of that. So let's look at the rumors at work in the story, address the rumors outside the story, and then follow Jesus' lead to see how she transcends them and shares a new story.

The rumors about this woman are hidden in some of the strangely specific details in this passage, most notably that she is getting water at noon. Noon is a very unusual time to get water. Most of the women going to the well would come in the early part of the day or near evening. They would do so first because it would not be as hot to carry the water jugs then, and arriving in the morning means you would have water to work with all day. So this woman, for some reason, is coming to the well at a time when no one else would be here. The implication is that she is not welcome to be at the well during the usual time. The other women must believe things about her that keep her isolated.

We might reason that some of the stories the women know about her concern her having had five husbands and now living with a man who is not her husband. Now, why can we assume that such a detail is general knowledge?

Jesus' response may contain a clue. The Bible gives us little emotional detail about how words on a page were delivered, so we cannot tell what sort of response the woman has to Jesus announcing that he knows about the men in her life. It is possible that the woman does not respond with shock that Jesus knows such information. She doesn't ask him how he knows this about her. Now, we might notice that her response to his declaration is to say, "Sir, I see you are a prophet." Such a sentence could imply that he has some supernatural knowledge about her that others don't. However, nothing in the text directly states amazement in her sentence. Sometimes I think there is even a bit of sarcasm in her words, "Oh, yes, you know all about me—you must be a prophet," even as she thinks, "Of course he knows that about me. Who doesn't?"

But maybe she is truly amazed at his knowledge, particularly because he is a stranger. She is, however, well-versed in deflecting those details about herself. She doesn't try to explain. She doesn't try to justify. She doesn't try to change the narrative. She has come to terms with her story and what it means for her life now. No sense defending, just keep coming to the well at noon instead of in the morning.

The details about her many husbands likely led to rumors about her in her day. But that same detail continues to haunt her memory. If you have studied this woman or heard a sermon about her, you have probably heard her characterized as a loose woman, an adulteress, a whore, or a prostitute at some point. Why? Because surely a good woman would be able to hold onto one husband and wouldn't be passed around by so many men, right?

It is tragic how often struggles in women's stories are

presumed to be sexual in nature. This is certainly true of women in the Bible. The same charge of prostitution is leveled at the woman in Luke 7, but all we are told about her is that she is a sinner, and she is from the city. Are women only allowed to partake in sexual sins? Can't she be a thief or a murderer? She has to be a prostitute? When it comes to the **Woman at the Well**, the charge of prostitution doesn't really make sense—at least for most of her story—since she was married, and there is no textual evidence that she was a prostitute. What if we tell a different story about her? What if we imagine she was a widow five times over? If she had lost five husbands, it is possible she just did not have the capacity to grieve another one, even as she still needed to be provided for, or it is possible that she was viewed as cursed, which could result in no man wanting to marry her and people talking about her at the well. It is also very possible that she was barren. Barrenness was a reason for someone to divorce you. It was also a reason for someone never to marry you in the first place, especially in that time and place. We could be much more charitable to this woman than we typically are, but instead, we tend to jump to the most salacious rumor and make it the truth. Honestly, that says more about who we are than who she is.

But here's the thing. Whether she was a widow, or childless, or a prostitute, for that matter, Jesus doesn't care. After he shares with her that he knows about her situation, he lets her steer the conversation away from those details. He doesn't say, "Hang on a second, we haven't dealt with the fact that you have all these men in your life. I need you to confess about that to me before we go any further." Nope. He just goes in the direction she takes the conversation, which is into a theological debate! As they discuss what it means to truly worship God, she shares her reflections toe-to-toe with his. She ends up having the longest single conversation that Jesus has with anyone in the entire Bible!

And then he confesses to her that he is the Messiah.

Up to this point, other people have proclaimed Jesus as the Son of God or the Lamb of God (see Chapter 1 for John the Baptist's and Nathaniel's declarations). In the previous chapter in John's Gospel, where Jesus is also having a theological debate with Nicodemus, Jesus is inviting Nicodemus to make the leap and understand who Jesus is saying he is, but this great teacher of Israel doesn't take the hint. However, this woman leads Jesus right up to the water, and he lets her drink! She is the first person in the Gospel of John to whom Jesus directly reveals that he is the Messiah.

Then this woman, who was and continues to be burdened by her own story—fairly or unfairly—runs off to tell a new story. She shares the good news of Jesus Christ. And beautifully, she uses her own story to get people to pay attention to what she is saying about him: "Many Samaritans from that city believed in him because of the woman's testimony, 'He told me everything I have ever done'" (John 4:39, NRSVue). She took her story, one that had been twisted and used to hold her down and allowed it to set everyone else free.

So if you find yourself oppressed by your own story—the one you tell yourself or the one others tell about you—put the rumors either to rest or to work as you come to the well with Jesus, drink deeply, and find some new good news to share in the way that only you can.

Prayer:

Lord, you see beyond the whispers and judgments we use to isolate and condemn each other. Let me live into the beloved image of God you see in me and then let me share that love abundantly and bravely with others. Amen.

Reflection Questions:

1. This chapter invites us to distinguish between what the biblical text actually says about the Samaritan woman and the stories or assumptions we often add to it. What "rumors" or assumptions about this woman have you heard or carried yourself, and how does rereading the text with fresh eyes challenge or reshape those assumptions?

2. Jesus names the woman's life circumstances but does not interrogate, shame, or require confession before engaging her in a deep theological conversation. What does Jesus' approach teach us about how God deals with our stories—and how might it change the way we treat others whose stories are already burdened by judgment or gossip?

3. The woman takes a story that has isolated her and uses it as the very means by which others come to believe. Can you think of ways your own story—especially the parts shaped by misunderstanding, pain, or labels—might become a source of connection or good news rather than shame? What would it take to tell that story differently?

About the Writer:

Michelle J. Morris is an ordained elder in the Arkansas Conference of The United Methodist Church and is the lead pastor of First United Methodist Church in downtown Bentonville, Arkansas. She is the author of *Gospel Discipleship: Four Pathways of Christian Discipleship* and *Prophets to the Generations.*

CHAPTER THIRTEEN

A Woman in the Village

By Kristin Joyner

Scripture Lesson: Acts 9:36-43

> *Now in Joppa there was a disciple whose name was Tabitha, which in Greek is Dorcas. She was devoted to good works and acts of charity. At that time she became ill and died. When they had washed her, they laid her in a room upstairs. Since Lydda was near Joppa, the disciples, who heard that Peter was there, sent two men to him with the request, "Please come to us without delay." So Peter got up and went with them, and when he arrived, they took him to the room upstairs. All the widows stood beside him, weeping and showing tunics and other clothing that Dorcas had made while she was with them. Peter put all of them outside, and then he knelt down and prayed. He turned to the body and said, "Tabitha, get up." Then she opened her eyes, and seeing Peter, she sat up. He gave her his hand and helped her up. Then calling the saints and widows, he showed her to be alive. This became known throughout Joppa, and many believed in the Lord. Meanwhile, he stayed in Joppa for some time with a certain Simon, a tanner.*
>
> **Acts 9:36-43 (NRSV)**

She never drove a car. That is what surprised me at a recent memorial for a mother of seven children. As is the case at many celebrations of a person's life, we heard stories about this woman—a mother, grandmother, and friend. Stories of a woman firmly engaged for decades in a community. A woman who probably wasn't perfect but was fondly remembered for her devotion to her family and church, her happy hours with friends, and her gift of retelling details about someone's life. In many ways, it seemed a quiet life, and I know that probably isn't what it felt like. A mother who traded babysitting and favors for carpooling, getting the family members to soccer and swimming, parties and events, catechism and youth group, while also supporting the PTA and Catholic charities. In all likelihood, she probably never described her life as quiet.

As well, there were things that weren't said. She wasn't famous. She wasn't an executive or a highly paid athlete. I have no idea whether she was on any social media platforms trying to get clicks, likes, and follows, whether she was ever in a news story, or whether she won any awards. It's possible, but none of that was mentioned at the celebration of her life. It was the quiet things, the things that society doesn't loudly celebrate, that were noticed and that were the highlights of her life to those around her. What always touches me is that when a person's life is over, it is the small, simple things that seem to matter most to those left behind. It is the gentle, quiet ways that a person lived, the very personal interactions that hold value beyond their earthly presence.

For many women, historically and in the present day, while lives vary, much time is spent on things that aren't typically described as exciting. Life and work can be quiet, consistent, and steady, even monotonous and boring. Women's lives are full of things that are necessary, foundational, and also unrequited. Much of our time is spent doing things that can feel unnoticed, hidden, or ignored. Most of us don't spend much time being big, loud, well-known, and overpaid. In a society where it's easy to feel lost among the noise, this is a reminder that likes, clicks, and follows don't truly measure value or worth, and that we can't measure worth by paychecks either. In truth, as Christians, we learn that our worth isn't measured at all; it just *is*. For most of us, our lives don't bring fame and wealth, but our recognition and worth are embedded as an integral part of God's creation. That is where we find our value.

When you think back to the stories of the Bible and the stories that we remember from Sunday school, how many of those stories are about women? We think about Noah, Moses, Job, Jonah, and Shadrach, Meshach, and Abednego. We think about Daniel, Jacob, Joshua, David, Solomon, Zacchaeus, and Lazarus.

But today, think about a woman: Tabitha, a woman in the village of Joppa.

A woman so beloved by her community, even as a widow, Tabitha was important enough for Peter to come to her home and resurrect her from the dead. She was resurrected! This resurrection story should easily be in the top ten—it is a statement about love and grace, worthiness, belonging, and overcoming death. It means "we need you," "we love you," "you are beloved." It means a story that lives beyond death!

Tabitha knew her people and took care of them. She was always doing good and helping the poor. She was a seamstress, likely one of many in the village. The robes and clothing that she made for the poor women in the community were so beautiful and special that women brought them to show Peter. "Look!" they said, "she cared about us, knew what we needed, and made us feel loved, made us feel like we belonged! We need more Tabitha!" I hope that Tabitha knew of their affection before her death.

I was actively growing into adulthood in the 1980s. In that time, women were joining the professional workforce in higher numbers than in years prior. Women were told they could do it all, have it all, be anything they wanted. And women were increasingly dressing in suits and ties. To belong in the workforce, many women felt they had to change who they were, somehow morphing into men to succeed. It was as if our value would be increased only so much as we became more "man-like." That was because it was in our paychecks where we would find our value. The reality of "be anything you want" and "I belong in the workforce" was easy to say, but the reality was closer to "become like a man if you want your value to increase."

When I saw the movie *Wonder Woman* in 2017, I cried. I didn't understand why, until I realized that I was finally seeing, for the first time, that women belonged in the realm of superheroes as superstars on the big screen! It was visceral, an "AHA!" moment, if you will. All the movies I had loved, and that the public has loved since movies have been movies, were based on men's stories, with men as the main characters. Women were always the secondary characters—usually with lines amid a crisis like, "What do we do now?!" with an answer from a heroic man always at the ready. It seemed that women were valued only to the extent that they supported a man's role. Now, that's an old trope, I know, but it is that sense that value comes from an outward place. This, we know, is not true. Women have had to work hard to discover or remember that value and worth don't come from a place of societal power, nor a paycheck.

This story of Tabitha being resurrected from the dead appears in the Book of Acts amid a long series of Peter, Paul, and the other apostles moving through the region, with act after act of healing. Just before this story, Peter heals a man who had been paralyzed for eight years, and all who witnessed this miraculous act convert to this New Way. It would be easy to read this story of Tabitha and move on quickly. It's just one more story of a healing act to help people believe in the power of Peter, Paul, and the other apostles. It's just one more story about how to get people to convert. But to do that would miss an important point.

This story comes at a time when the movement is growing, drawing people together to hear about this new way of being—the way of following Jesus. The movement is working to expand the welcome and belonging beyond societal expectations about who is valued and worthy. Her story, our Scripture says, "became known throughout Joppa" (Acts 9:42). Imagine that story—a woman seamstress is resurrected from the dead! What were the people saying in tea houses and villages?

"Who was she? Was she famous? She must have been famous! Someone important! Was she a queen?"

"No, just a seamstress."

"Why was she so important? Why her? Why would a Jew care about her?"

"She was just a woman."

"There's a God that will do that for a woman—a regular woman, not even from that tribe and who is just a seamstress!?"

It must have been truly astounding. Joppa was a Gentile area; it was not Jewish. This movement is developing the early church and beginning to include people beyond the Jewish population. This New Way includes ALL people.

There was not just an increase in the number of followers, but an increase in diversity and inclusion of non-Aramaic speakers and speakers of all languages. We know that Stephen and others were intentionally chosen to include the widows and orphans of the Greek-speaking Hellenists in their care. Philip had gone to the unfavored area of Samaria to heal and grow the church there. They traveled to a faraway region and met the Ethiopian eunuch. This was someone who was clearly not a Jew but was valued enough that, after learning about Jesus, he was baptized by Philip. These are all people who had been shunned and deemed less important, but now it is clear that they have inherent worth and must be included in the church!

In the formation of the church, the inclusion of more and more people—especially those who have been excluded: the widows, the orphans, the Samaritans, and the eunuchs—is the New Way. All people are invited into belonging! All people are worthy, for exactly who they are. This invitation doesn't require changing identities or assimilating into one way of being; it recognizes that a person's value lies in their very being, who God created them to be.

In the Book of Luke, there are more stories of women as disciples, women of prominence, and women as supporters of Jesus' ministries than in the other Gospels. The Book of Acts, written by the same author, continues that narrative, referring to the women who were disciples and part of the mission stories. In the years since the writings of Luke and Acts, the importance and value of women have been alternately diminished, forgotten, argued, and reclaimed. This is why it is important to remember Tabitha.

It is hard not to be amazed by a story of resurrection, but the story of Tabitha really shouldn't surprise us. In 1 Kings 17:17-24, Elijah, and in 2 Kings 4, Elisha, each resurrect a child from death at the request of a woman. Although their names are unknown, these women were important enough in their time—and influential enough as women—for us to hear their stories of resurrection.

When Peter heard about Tabitha, he didn't question whether she was worthy of this small miracle; he knew that her value and worth were held by God, as simple as that. When the author of this story retells what happened, Tabitha's name is carefully presented in both Aramaic (Tabitha) and Greek (Dorcas). Why does the author do this? The message of love and acceptance is not just for Aramaic-speaking Jews; the message of welcome and belonging is also for Greek-speaking people.

This growth of the church was an important evolution in spreading the good news beyond the Jewish population because it represented a revolutionary way of seeing people. No longer would people need to be divided or "othered." People have inherent worth and must be valued because they are part of God's own creation—not because they are Jewish, circumcised, or men. God doesn't value people the way society does; societal standards don't measure value.

Tabitha (Dorcas) was a simple woman by many measures. She made clothes. She wasn't famous, at least not at the time. She wasn't an important political figure or decorated warrior. She most certainly wasn't on any social media platform getting clicks, likes, and follows, and not much else about her is known. What was important enough for us to know was her value to the community. This woman, in her care for others, in the simple use of her talents as a seamstress, held such worth and value that we know her story today. Peter knew her value at the time and brought her back to life, back among the community that loved her so much.

At the end of this Scripture passage, there's a short sentence: "He stayed in Joppa for some time with a certain Simon, a tanner." This detail is important and intentional. Tanners touch dead animal skin and were considered ceremonially unclean. This detail reminds us that "uncleanliness" in people doesn't exist. Even the tanner is valued.

Our church, from the very beginning, calls us to value and claim importance for those that society pushes aside. We are called to value and place worth on the everyday people, the people who quietly share their gifts and talents, those who care about building and supporting community, carpooling, babysitting, and getting kids to soccer practice. God created—and continues to create—a beautiful diversity of people: women, men, eunuchs, Samaritans, tanners, widows, and orphans, to name just a few.

Imagine a society that doesn't wait until a celebration of life to remind people of their worthiness and value. Imagine if we reminded people every day that their small, daily ways of *being* matter! Imagine a life in which you are reminded every day that small and quiet—even boring—things matter. We can move away from the common misperception that value and worth are placed only on ways of being that are big and loud, on the famous and the rich. Our value and worth come from who God is, not from what we do or how loudly we do it. We know this to be true, and yet it is easy to forget.

Tabitha is a woman who mattered because of *who God is*, not because of her fame or wealth. She quietly used her gifts to make clothes and care for her neighbors, living into God's vision of beloved community. This is where true value and worthiness are found.

May it be so.

Prayer:

Creative and Creating God, we give you thanks for the gifts of a woman named Tabitha, also known as Dorcas, and for all the women who have gone before us and for those still to come who care for community in small yet generous ways. May we be the people who live into the vision for loving our neighbors in our everyday lives, knowing that even small and simple things matter to you. May we be the people who remind others of their value and their worthiness because of who you are and who you created and are creating us to be. Amen.

Reflection Questions:

1. What are your simple, everyday gifts? Do you know that God placed those gifts in you to build community? How do you use those gifts?

2. Think of a person in your life who does simple, meaningful things regularly. Find ways to thank and appreciate them as a person created by God for that purpose. Don't wait for their memorial service.

3. How is value shown in our society, and how can we be a part of doing that better?

About the Writer:

Kristin Joyner serves as pastor of Community Engagement at Bothell United Methodist Church in Washington State. She is passionate about letting the local community know that the church is a place of inclusion, living and learning the life of Jesus, so that we can boldly advocate for loving justice.

CHAPTER FOURTEEN

Female Church Planters of the New Testament

By Rev. Rachel Gilmore

Scripture Lessons:

Romans 16:7, Acts 16:13-15, Acts 18:24-26, Romans 16:1-2, Colossians 4:15, Philippians 4:2-3

Greet Andronicus and Junia, my fellow Jews who have been in prison with me. They are outstanding among the apostles, and they were in Christ before I was.

Romans 16:7 (NIV)

On the Sabbath we went outside the city gate to the river, where we expected to find a place of prayer. We sat down and began to speak to the women who had gathered there. One of those listening was a woman from the city of Thyatira named Lydia, a dealer in purple cloth. She was a worshiper of God. The Lord opened her heart to respond to Paul's message. When she and the members of her household were baptized, she invited us to her home. "If you consider me a believer in the Lord," she said, "come and stay at my house." And she persuaded us.

Acts 16:13-15 (NIV)

Meanwhile a Jew named Apollos, a native of Alexandria, came to Ephesus. He was a learned man, with a thorough knowledge of the Scriptures. He had been instructed in the way of the Lord, and he spoke with great fervor and taught about Jesus accurately, though he knew only the baptism of John. He began to speak boldly in the synagogue. When Priscilla and Aquila heard him, they invited him to their home and explained to him the way of God more adequately.

Acts 18:24-26 (NIV)

I commend to you our sister Phoebe, a deacon of the church in Cenchreae. I ask you to receive her in the Lord in a way worthy of his people and to give her any help she may need from you, for she has been the benefactor of many people, including me.

Romans 16:1-2 (NIV)

Give my greetings to the brothers and sisters at Laodicea, and to Nympha and the church in her house.

Colossians 4:15 (NIV)

I plead with Euodia and I plead with Syntyche to be of the same mind in the Lord. Yes, and I ask you, my true companion, help these women since they have contended at my side in the cause of the gospel, along with Clement and the rest of my co-workers, whose names are in the book of life.

Philippians 4:2-3 (NIV)

I was scared to death when I showed up at the church-planting training in Dallas, Texas, with my six-month-old son. I was a twenty-eight-year-old, first-time mother in my first appointment to plant a United Methodist church in Virginia Beach, and I had no idea what I was doing. I met one of the facilitators at the door, and he smiled warmly as he said, "I'm so glad you are here, but I want you to know that very few women plant churches, and young moms *don't* plant churches. So learn what you can, but don't beat yourself up if it doesn't work out." While he might have intended to be kind, the words cut like a knife. The bishop and cabinet discerned me for this position, and I was already feeling defeated!

My mother was ordained in the American Baptist Church in the 1970s, so I'd seen women lead the church my whole life, but could God use a woman to start a church? Didn't the apostles in the New Testament start the churches, and weren't they all guys? Would this work? Was this part of God's plan?

What does Scripture say? What do the women in Scripture say?

Lindsay Hardin Freeman is an Episcopal priest who spent three years with a team from her church looking at every recorded word that a woman spoke in the Bible, and they found that out of the estimated 1.1 million words of Scripture, ninety-three women speak a combined 14,000 words (which is around 1.2% of Scripture). And when I looked at the New Testament to see if a female church planter spoke any words, there were none. Those harsh realities resonated with me, leading to greater feelings of isolation and imposter syndrome. And then I was reminded of the words that Moravian church leader Peter Boehler spoke to a young and discouraged John Wesley hundreds of years ago during a crisis of call. Peter said, "Preach faith until you have it, and then because you have it, you will preach faith." With Boehler's advice, I preached, taught, and reached out to other young moms, young adults, and young families in my community, believing that God could call men AND women to start churches.

Within seven months, we launched worship in the gym of an existing church, and seven months after that, we launched a worship service at a downtown theater with over one hundred people in attendance at our first service. The church grew to hundreds of people connected to our ministries and attending on Sunday mornings over the next ten years, while I had the honor and privilege of serving one of the most incredible churches I have ever known.

And over that time, as I dug more deeply into God's word, I noticed that while female church planters don't speak in the New Testament, they were present and had a profound impact on the early church. At least seven female church planters are mentioned in the New Testament, and they all share the **power of being seen, the power of place, and the power of a name**. From Junia to Phoebe, Priscilla to Lydia, and brief references to Nympha, Euodia, and Syntyche, just the fact that these women are named in light of their roles in starting or building early churches is significant. In a culture where women were considered property and not guaranteed the ability to read—let alone lead a church—just *seeing* the names of these women is a reminder to me that women in ministry aren't mythical unicorns; they do exist and have existed for thousands of years.

There was a time when the male-dominated church sought to erase women's names from God's word. Medieval Christianity was so threatened by the thought of a female apostle that they encouraged theologians like Martin Luther to change the biblical translation of the name Junia to Junius, erasing the woman's gender in Romans 16:7, where she is listed as "prominent among the apostles." So not only was Junia an apostle, but she also stood out among the crowd of her apostles with her husband, Andronicus. St. John Chrysostom was an "early church father" who served as the archbishop of Constantinople in the 4th century. Chrysostom acknowledged that Junia, a woman, was an apostle and also spoke of the women Euodia and Syntyche as the heads of the church in Philippi. Nympha is listed in Colossians 4:15 as being the head of a house church. Sometimes just showing up and being seen, being named in a space, is a way we can live into our calling.

But these women also had the power of *place*. What do I mean by that? Well, when the apostle Paul meets Priscilla and her husband, Aquilla, in Corinth as tentmakers, he builds a relationship with them, and soon they are all traveling to Ephesus and then Rome together to continue the work of church planting. And when this church-planting couple is mentioned in Scripture, Priscilla's name comes first, which is highly unusual and can demonstrate that she was the more revered or renowned church planter of the two. We go on to read that Paul asks Priscilla and Aquila to help provide a theological foundation for Apollos when his teaching goes off the rails, and that Priscilla helps shape the male leaders of the early church through proper instruction. When Andronicus and his wife, Junia, are mentioned as respected apostles in Romans 16:7, we read that they had been imprisoned with Paul. So Junia's power of place was being locked up for her faith, as was the case with the other apostles, and she continued to proclaim the good news. Lydia is another house church leader mentioned in Acts 16:14-15 as the first woman baptized in Europe after she met Paul in Philippi. Lydia would go on to host a house church and use her place of prominence as a wealthy businesswoman to share the good news with her network of personal and professional friends throughout the city.

Finally, these female church planters had the power of a *name*. In Greco-Roman times and throughout Judaism, your name was a prophecy over who you would become or what you would do. Culturally, women played a key role in naming their children. So women shaped the names of Junia (youthful goddess of women and childbirth), Lydia (noble one from a place of wealth and kings), Priscilla (ancient and venerable), Phoebe (bright, pure, radiant), Euodia (good way), Syntyche (with fortune, chance, fate), and Nympha (bride or young wife). These women and their names serve as a reminder to us that when we are faithful to the call of God on our lives, we too can become noble, radiant, and venerated leaders—women who birth new churches as the bride of Christ, following in the good way and living out our calling in new and faithful ways.

I thought of the legacy passed on from generation to generation in the naming of children as I held my second child in my arms, born the day after my first Easter service at this new church plant. I named her Elizabeth, after my Italian grandmother who taught me more about faith than anyone I've ever known. Elizabeth is a biblical name (John the Baptist's mother was also Elizabeth), and it comes from two Hebrew words meaning "God is my oath" or "God's promise." Holding her and celebrating new life in this new faith community reminded me that God's promise to be with us, to see us, to give us a place and a purpose of sharing the good news with the world is the greatest gift we will ever receive. God's oath of love is something we can build our lives on and around as we continue to break down preconceived notions about what women can and cannot do and how we can and cannot serve.

Prayer:

God, when I feel unseen or unimportant in the eyes of the world, help me to remember that you see me, and you have given me a place and a purpose in your loving kin-dom. When the world tells me I can't do something, may I turn to you for next steps and follow your way with grit and grace.

Reflection Questions:

1. Have you ever shown up in a space where you didn't feel like you belonged? How does belonging to Christ help us in those spaces?

2. Have you ever felt like the patriarchy in the church has tried to minimize or change your name or role in the church in ways that God wouldn't? How can we stand in our calling when society is uncomfortable with it?

3. What is your name? Does it hold significance for you? Have you ever named someone? What went into your decision?

About the Writer:

Rachel Gilmore serves as the director of New and Vital Faith in the Desert Southwest Conference of The United Methodist Church. She lives with her family in Phoenix where she also co-founded Intersect: a Church-Planting Network.

www.ingramcontent.com/pod-product-compliance
Lightning Source LLC
LaVergne TN
LVHW010925110826
845149LV00013B/2483